IMPLANT RETAINED PROSTHESES: SCREW VERSUS CEMENT

SURABHI DUGGAL | SAHIL THAKAR |
MANSIMRANJIT KAUR UPPAL

ISBN 979-888569519-0

Contents

Prologue

- Introduction
- Rationale for implants
- Surgical guidelines for implant placement
- Immediate implant placement
- Impression techniques for implant dentistry
- Screw and cement-retained restorations
- Some situations prefer one method of retention over another
- Screw retained crown restorations of single implants
- Cement retained implant prosthesis
- Method for registering the abutment screw position of cement-retained implant restorations
- Technique for retrieving cement-retained implant prosthesis
- Complications
- Conclusion
- Summary
- References

Long-term success is the prime goal for any restoration in prosthetic treatment and so is it with implant dentistry. Implant dentistry has seen rapid and remarkable progress in recent years. The quest for predictable long term results has raised several questions concerning the techniques followed in clinical practice. Also, implants placed during the development era had high failure rates and therefore, easy and frequent removal of the prostheses was important. The choice of the restorative components and the connection system between the implants and the restorations must be considered a paramount factor. The majority of the systems available today offer different types of connections between prosthetic restorations and supporting implants.

According to GPT 9, implant prosthodontics is the selection, planning, development, placement, replacement of missing teeth and/ or associated structures, and maintenance of restoration(s) with dental implants.

Implant restorations can be screw-retained, cement-retained or a combination of both.

Screw retention in implant-supported prostheses was developed in response to the need for retrievability and the simplicity of replacement and maintenance of both the restorations and the implants, making the evaluation of oral hygiene and peri-implant probing easier, even though occlusion and esthetics were compromised. As techniques advanced, implant survival rates moved rapidly from the 50% to the 90% range, but the use of screw retention still remains the retention mechanism of choice.

Cement-retained prostheses have superior occlusion, esthetics (due to the absence of the occlusal access hole, the use of angled and individualized abutments and the use of less expensive components and restorative procedures), passivity (the cement layer compensates for incidental dimensional discrepancies between the abutment and the restoration working as a shock absorber and uniformly transferring loads to the implant–prosthesis–bone complex) and loading characteristics when compared with screw-retained prostheses. Cement, when used appropriately, can retain implant-supported prostheses and provide retrievability. It has been used in fixed prosthodontics for almost 100 years and has a significant and well-documented history. The main disadvantage is the difficulty of their retrievability for oral hygiene, peri-implant tissues monitoring and replacement or maintenance of prosthetic components. In order to maintain the possible retrievability of such restorations, the use of temporary luting agents has been suggested for the cementation of restorations. After the cementation procedure excess removal of the luting agent can be difficult and the permanency of residual cement in the soft tissues can result in peri-implant inflammation.

The choice of cement-retained or screw-retained implants has a major impact on the final occlusal design and directly affects the force transmitted to the components and the bone-implant interface. The attachment mechanisms of cement retention and screw retention are dramatically different. In screw-retained restorations, the fastening screw provides a solid joint between the restoration and the implant abutment, while in cement-retained prostheses the restorative screw is eliminated to enhance esthetics, occlusal stability, and passive fit of the restorations.

However, screw-retained restorative systems are prone to mechanical complications increasing the rate of screw loosening and fractures. It has been reported to occur in 6–48% of the restorations. Moreover, replacing implant screws is very expensive due to the cost of the components. The presence of the access screw hole interferes with a natural occlusal morphology and induces screw and abutment loosening.

Cement-retained restorations are not affected by the strain on implants caused by the screw. The absence of passive fit of screw connection turns even small dimensional discrepancies into static loads, resulting in mechanical deformations and stress concentration on the implants.

ONE

The clinical replacement of lost natural teeth by implants is one of the most significant advances in dentistry. Earlier many dentists were sceptical about implants and rejected them today it is rare to find a practitioner who does not work with implants.

Compared to all other fields, implant dentistry has gained more innovation and development in recent years. New improved diagnostic and technical procedures have also advanced from the introduction of CAD-CAM technology to improve the precision of fit and allow restoration of implants in non-ideal positions. Today clinicians can prescribe the use of implants with the knowledge and confidence that they will predictably integrate into the jaw bone. In order to claim success, the definitive restorations must restore the patient to normal contour, function, aesthetics, speech and health

Implants have many advantages over conventional fixed or removable treatment options and in many cases is the treatment of choice. This is a result of many factors which can be divided into four categories:

1. Preservation of tooth structure
2. Preservation of bone
3. Provision of additional support
4. Resistance to disease.

PRESERVATION OF TOOTH STRUCTURE

Fixed partial dentures have been considered the standard before implants, but a significant amount of tooth structure needs to be removed for an aesthetic outcome. This compromises the longevity of the tooth and can result in endodontic, periodontal and mechanical complications.

Teeth that are pulp capped are at high risk for requiring endodontic therapy and making poor choices for abutment teeth and reducing the long term stability of an FPD.

In comparison to other prosthetic designs, implant single-tooth implant had the lowest failure rate and is the most predictable method of tooth replacement. No reports of loss of adjacent teeth have been undertaken; this is different to when treatment is rendered with an FPD which 6 may require the span to be extended further, when the adjacent teeth are unprepared and exhibit large pulp chambers thus further compromising the long term stability of the prosthesis.

PRESERVATION OF BONE

There is a close relationship between the tooth and the alveolar process throughout life. Bone requires stimulation to maintain its form and density. When a tooth is lost, the lack of stimulation to the residual bone causes a decrease in trabeculae and bone density in the area, with loss in height and width. In the edentulous patient, the bone tends to resorb upwards and medially in the maxilla and downwards and laterally in the mandible. This often results in a jaw size discrepancy which tends more toward a class 3 skeletal relationship. To respect this natural disproportion, teeth must be aligned differently with the maxillary molars being more facially positioned and the mandibular molars being more lingually positioned.

The literature concludes that teeth are required to maintain bone and with loss of teeth, bone is no longer stimulated. A partial or complete denture does not maintain the bone and may accelerate bone loss if the prosthesis is ill-fitting. Continued bone loss decreases the surface area available for prosthesis support, eliminates favourable anatomy for retention and results in unfavourable denture bearing areas. Loss of lateral stability and retention increases prosthesis movement resulting in increased friction and mucosal irritation. The bone loss can be so severe that even if the patient desires implant therapy there may not be sufficient bone and would require grafting. Together with bone loss are associated soft tissue changes which can significantly affect the overall aesthetics. Facial changes that occur as a result of ageing are accelerated with the loss of teeth. The loss of facial support and reduction in vertical dimension gives the appearance of the denture patient who presents with a decreased nose to chin distance, deepening of the labiomental fold and thinning of the vermillion border of the lips. These biological changes can be avoided by the placement of implants which will stimulate the bone and avoid subsequent resorption.

PROVISION OF ADDITIONAL SUPPORT

Additional support can be provided with the use of dental implants, which improves masticatory performance. The maximum occlusal force in an edentulous patient can be 7 reduced to 50 psi, the longer a patient is edentulous the less force they are able to generate. Restoring a patient's stomatognathic system to a more normal function may enhance their masticatory performance and improve their quality of life. Transitioning a patient from a complete denture to implant-supported fixed prosthesis results in a dramatic increase in maximal bite force. The improved stability and retention of an implant-supported prosthesis is a vast improvement on soft tissue supported dentures. Patients also present clinically with one or more signs of lack of posterior support. These signs may include but are not limited to wear, splaying and fremitus of the anterior teeth

An advantage of implant-supported restorations is retrievability. Implant restorations can be screw-retained, cement-retained or a combination of the two. Screw retained prostheses can easily be retrieved than cemented. Retrievability is advantageous for the replacement or salvaging of the restoration. Many problems can arise such as

1. Loosening of the retaining screw
2. Fracture of porcelain
3. Fracture of an abutment
4. Modification of the prosthesis through loss of an implant.

RESISTANCE TO DISEASE

Recurrent caries can occur beneath restorations, at the margins of restorations or on the root surfaces. An assessment of disease susceptibility and control is essential prior to formulate a definitive treatment plan. Root surface caries is prevalent amongst the elderly population and is associated with the reduced salivary flow resulting from many drugs prescribed for patients in this age group. In patients who are disease susceptible, often decisions need to be made with regards to preserving teeth or choosing a more predictable long term option by the placement of dental implants.

Patients wearing removable partial dentures often exhibit greater mobility of the abutment teeth, greater plaque retention, increased bleeding on probing, more incidence of caries and accelerated bone loss in the edentulous regions. Implants are not susceptible to dental caries and can preserve adjacent teeth. Often decisions need to be made as to when extraction and implant placement is a feasible option. A thorough risk analysis must be performed

TWO

SURGICAL GUIDELINES FOR IMPLANT PLACEMENT

The goal of an implant-supported reconstruction is to obtain optimal aesthetics and function. To achieve this, visualisation of the final restoration is necessary prior to beginning treatment. The term 'restorative-driven' treatment planning has been used to identify this process. It requires a team approach of specialists, who can develop a multidisciplinary treatment plan, starting with an accurate diagnosis, which will lead to a prognosis of each individual tooth and the overall dentition. This information will help the clinician develop the treatment options suitable for tooth replacement.

Effective communication between the team and the patient is important. Understanding the patient's expectations is key to a successful outcome. Deciding that these expectations are realistic requires a correct diagnosis and an inter-disciplinary treatment plan. This approach takes time and requires a comprehensive treatment discussion between the team members, and then a thorough case presentation to the patient. Only then will the patient begin to understand the extent of their problem and the options available to reconstruct their mouth.

All the treating specialists on the team need to collaborate their findings, which includes the following examinations:

A. Periodontal examination

A comprehensive periodontal examination includes the soft and hard supporting tissues of the dentition. The patient's tissue biotype is classified according to how thick or thin the supporting bone and gingival soft tissues are defined. If periodontal disease is present, it is important to establish the attachment level (probing depths and gingival recession) and any contributing factors, such as mucogingival problems (lack of keratinised attached tissue) and furcation involvement, which will alter the prognosis of the remaining teeth. It is critical to identify the level of the crestal alveolar bone. The normal crest is defined as 2 mm from the CEJ and the low crest is present in patients with recession. Sounding to bone is the best clinical parameter to help identify the attachment level, this is important in the aesthetic zone when considering replacing partially edentulous teeth. The interproximal attachment level on the teeth adjacent to a future implant site will dictate the future gingival architecture. In the aesthetic zone, it is important to identify the number of teeth and soft tissues visible from the frontal and lateral view, both with the lip at rest and when smiling. Un-even gingival architecture, the position of teeth relative to the arch shape and opposing occlusion will affect and dictate the decision making process. The presence of bone loss due to periodontal disease or trauma will greatly affect the outcome of treatment. If teeth are already missing then the amount of ridge collapse needs to be measured according to both horizontal and vertical collapse. If the prognosis of teeth is deemed hopeless due to periodontal, endodontic or nonrestorability factors, then anticipating the amount of future ridge collapse needs to be estimated. Deciding when to extract a tooth is easy when it is hopeless, but often more heroic attempts to save teeth that are broken down with a questionable prognosis is not as simple. In order to preserve the alveolar bone for implants, sacrificing teeth (early extraction) requires a change of thinking as compared to previous philosophical treatment decisions. B. Occlusal analysis Patients with parafunctional habits will greatly affect the outcome and longevity of the type of reconstruction planned. In the periodontally compromised patient, loss of teeth without replacement leads to lack of posterior support. This often causes an unstable occlusal scheme with mesial drifting of posterior teeth and flaring of anterior teeth with a loss of vertical dimension. A full examination includes not only the mobility of remaining teeth, but also the occlusal scheme and guidance in lateral and protrusive movements. Over-eruption of any teeth will cause occlusal interferences and also decrease the inter-occlusal space necessary for implant restorative components. Lack of restorative space is a major contributor to mechanical failure of implant restorations. Mounted diagnostic casts are used to evaluate the occlusion, the edentulous space ridge relationship to the adjacent teeth and the opposing dentition. The amount of vertical and horizontal overlap, the restorative space available is important. Replacing teeth in partially edentulous spaces, without comprehensive care of the remaining dentition, will cause failure in the long term. C. Endodontic The endodontic integrity and vitality of remaining dentition must be established. Any periapical lesions and existing root canals that are incomplete need to be evaluated. Any teeth 10 with a poor endodontic prognosis should have a thorough risk assessment completed, so as not to jeopardise future implant sites. D. Restorative The integrity of all existing restorations should be evaluated. This must include margin integrity and soft tissue response to sub-gingival placement. Teeth with biologic width violation, that will require surgical crown lengthening, will affect the level of the osseous crest at sites adjacent to implants. The strategic value of each tooth needs to be determined, prior to removal. Often in complex cases, even teeth with a poor prognosis can be kept in the initial phases to support a fixed interim prosthesis, while implant healing progresses. This phased approach of sequential extraction will help manage the complex case, sometimes through long periods (two years) while site development and healing of implant sites is progressing. E. Orthodontic Analysis of the restorative space along with the position and angulation of the roots in the alveolar bone is important regarding future tooth restoration size. Drifting and tipping of remaining teeth present problems with space mesially-distally. The orthodontist needs to be given clear instructions when opening or closing spaces in regards to root positions. Taking radiographs during treatment will give useful information to the treating team, prior to appliance removal and completion of treatment. It is always preferable in aesthetic cases to complete the orthodontic care prior to implant placement. In cases missing posterior teeth, provisional interim implants can be placed to help the orthodontist establish anchorage. The final implants should only be placed posteriorly, if the orthodontic wax-up of the final result allows for correct positioning, without compromising the end result. F. Radiographic examination The preliminary exam will include a set of full mouth periapical and bitewing radiographs. A 3-D CT scan imaging will be used. 11 Once the patient has accepted the proposed options, a diagnostic wax-up of the final proposed treatment will be a template to fabricate a radiographic guide. This radiographic guide can be placed in the mouth at the time of the CT scan. Lack of bone and ridge collapse both horizontally and vertically can be accurately measured. The surgical needs can be identified and the most predictable options can be presented to the patient prior to beginning treatment. The goals of the final reconstruction, whether fixed or removable, can be determined. The treatment plan in a phased approach, all financial obligations, treatment consent as well as aesthetic goals are established prior to taking any further steps. Occasionally, when questionable teeth are still present, it may be beneficial to have a CT scan prior to removing teeth. This can help make treatment decisions regarding surgical options of timing of implant placement. Pre-surgical planning Viewing the CT images which have the cross sectional reformatted images of the bone quantity and quality at each desired implant site, allows the surgeon to develop the surgical plan. He can then modify the radiographic guide to be used as a surgical guide on the day of surgery. Recent developments in CAD-CAM technology allow the team to perform presurgical planning on a virtual model and then transfer this information to a clinical surgical guide to assist accurate placement of implants.

THREE

SURGICAL GUIDELINES — TOOTH OR TEETH ALREADY MISSING

Adequate osseous ridge

The Brånemark surgical protocol established osseointegration as an extremely predictable option for tooth replacement with excellent long term stability. It is important for all members of the team to discuss which components are to be used surgically and restoratively, so that the benefits and limitations are defined. Whether the prosthesis will be screw retained or cement retained can affect the axial inclination and angle of placement. Due to common anatomical limitations post-extraction (concavities and collapse of the ridge circumference), using cement retained restorations allows greater flexibility at the time of surgical placement.

Flap design

The original Brånemark protocol required a vestibular flap with a two-stage approach. The implant was placed and buried under the soft tissue and after an adequate period of healing (three months mandible, six months maxilla), a second stage surgery was performed with crestal incisions to expose the fixtures and connect a trans-epithelial abutment. After adequate soft tissue healing, the dentist could fabricate the prosthesis.

One stage surgical protocols allowed the implant fixture to extend through the soft tissues during the period of initial healing. This trend continues with most implants placed with a one-stage protocol allowing adequate time for healing prior to loading the fixtures. Using this technique requires a crestal incision or even a flapless approach, drilling directly through the soft tissues. Deciding which cases are suitable for the flapless technique is the key to a successful outcome; adequate bone width with plenty of keratinised soft tissue is desired. In the aesthetic zone, it is important to maintain adequate thickness on the buccal aspect of the implant for the long term stability of the soft tissue contours. Usually, this area lacks enough tissue due to resorption subsequent to tooth loss, and augmentation techniques are required. Using a two-stage protocol in the aesthetic zone also allows for an additional opportunity for surgical intervention with further hard or soft tissue grafting procedures. Langer introduced the sub-epithelial connective tissue graft as a predictable technique for augmenting thin tissue and it is especially useful when minor ridge resorption is present. The most common donor site is the palatal tissue mesial to the first molar. Another popular donor site is the tuberosity tissue. This area is especially desirable when a thicker graft is needed for ridge augmentation 13 procedures (inlay or pouch technique) in the anterior aesthetic zone. Palacci has described rotated flap techniques for papilla regeneration. It is important to define the type of defect, and realise that building the supporting bone beneath the soft tissue will produce the most predictable outcome. The bony architecture provides the scaffold that supports the soft tissue around proper implant positioning

POSITION AND ANGULATION OF IMPLANT

Presurgical analysis has determined the best available sites for placement. In the partially edentulous case, the root morphology and inclination of teeth adjacent to the implant site are crucial. If a radiographic guide was used at the time of CT scan and then adapted for use as a surgical guide, mishaps will be prevented. If a surgical guide is fabricated without the knowledge of the root positions or bony deficiencies, then careful interpretation and adjustments by the surgeon are required. The initial drilling (round bur) starting point can be moved and the angulation of the implant tipped to avoid bone dehiscence or fenestration. The more palatal the movement, the deeper sub-gingivally the implant platform must be positioned to accommodate for the emergence of the restorative components through the soft tissue. Ideal dimensions are 3–4 mm subgingival, with the buccal aspect of the implant platform at least 1 mm or more palatal or lingual to the future buccal aspect of the restoration at the level of the gingival margin.

SURGICAL GUIDELINES — TOOTH OR TEETH NEED TO BE REMOVED

If the tooth or teeth need to be removed, then ask the following questions.

- Is the tooth in the aesthetic zone?
- Type of tissue biotype? Thin scalloped or thick flat.
- Amount of bone loss due to periodontal disease or endodontic failure?
- How predictable is the stability of the future gingival architecture?

There are several timing options to consider:

1. Extract and wait several months prior to implant placement
2. Orthodontic forced eruption to move the gingival complex and crestal bone into a more favourable position prior to extraction
3. Extract and bone graft the socket to help preserve soft tissue contours and minimise the collapse of the ridge, if the buccal plate is thin or has slight dehiscence.
4. Extract and place an implant immediately into the socket

a. Two-stage buried.

b. One stage with healing abutment or customised healing abutment.

c. Immediate load implant with a provisional restoration.

5. Extract and wait two to three months, for soft tissue maturity then bone graft. After five to six months of healing, place the implant.

Timing of loading

Changing the implant surface from a smooth machined finish to a roughened surface has been shown to improve the rate of bone healing adjacent to the implant. This allows a quicker healing time for osseointegration to be established. With improved and modified drilling techniques, the primary stability of the implant at the time of placement has improved. This has led to immediate loading with provisional restorations at the time of placement. The primary factor for success at the time of placement is achieving primary stability. The recent development of the OsstellTM machine that quantifies stability of the fixture using sound resonance has helped to give an objective measurement to determine treatment outcomes. Any micro-motion during the initial phases of bone healing will cause a lack of integration. Failure is most often caused by overloading due to trans-mucosal forces of a removable appliance over the implant site. Any attempt to keep a patient functioning with fixed provisional restorations during the healing phases of treatment will allow for easier patient management. Transitional implants were developed to help support interim fixed or removable prostheses during the healing phases. These implants have also been used to support a surgical guide and have also been adapted to aid orthodontic treatment, where there is a lack of anchorage. If immediate loading at the time of final definitive implant placement is to be considered, not only should the initial stability be extremely tight, but control of the occlusion on the provisional interim restoration must be adjusted and monitored carefully 15 through the initial healing period. Single anterior teeth are best for immediate loading as compared to posterior teeth where the occlusal forces are greater. In fully edentulous cases, immediate loading with a rigid splinted interim prosthesis is advised. If predictability is desired in the aesthetic zone, treatment options that cut down on time and the number of procedures do not always produce the most reliable aesthetic results. This option increases the risk of failure and also makes it more difficult to predict the future level of the buccal tissue contours, due to shrinkage, but it supports the adjacent papilla.

Surgical complications

In order to minimise post-surgical complications, careful planning of the flap design, and gentle soft tissue manipulation is required. Control of bleeding, along with releasing incisions that allow for flap advancement and closure without tension is mandatory. Failure to maintain flap coverage due to sloughing or opening of the incision line will lead to delayed healing with compromised results. Smoking affects both hard and soft tissue healing and is the greatest risk factor. The medically compromised patient (eg Diabetes Mellitus, Autoimmune disease, patients on long term steroids, radiation treatment etc) needs special attention but is not contra-indicated to receiving treatment. Logical and ethical decisions need to be made with the patient and their physicians.

FOUR

IMMEDIATE IMPLANT PLACEMENT : PROSTHETIC PHASE

Dental implantation is considered the optimal procedure to restore dentition. This one-stage implantation is one of the most high demand dental procedure among patients nowadays. It helps to restore the defects of dentition during one procedure. The successful prosthetic phase on one-stage implant depends on adequate implant placement.

The prosthetic phase starts after 10 weeks since implant placement.

Once the decision has been made that the patient is a candidate for immediate implant placement, a surgical guide should be used to assure proper implant placement. A provisional appliance with an ovate pontic should be available for insertion after implant placement.

Tooth extraction and implant placement procedure :

The patient is anaesthetised and various flap procedures can be used to gain access for tooth extraction. Teeth to be removed and implants placed immediately after extraction can be accessed using either an open, flapped approach or with a minimally invasive technique. The surgeon can displace the marginal tissues buccal/lingually to gain access to the surgical site A Molt C2 (Hufriedy, Chicago) curette can be used to luxate the root mesial-distally. Care must be exercised not to luxate buccal-lingually. Excessive force in this direction can damage the buccal plate. After tooth removal, a curette is used to explore the location of the buccal plate and confirm that it is intact. The surgical guide is placed over the surgical site and a sharp Precision Drill is used to penetrate the palatal wall of the extraction socket. This drill guides the drills used to create the osteotomy. In the maxillary anterior region, it is important to avoid placing the implant directly into the extraction socket. Placement of the implant in this position will cause it to perforate the buccal plate and jeopardise implant survival. The axis of the implant must be even with the incisal edges of the adjacent teeth or slightly palatal to this landmark. A direction indicator should be used to verify the correct angulation and trajectory of the proposed implant. Standard drilling procedures are performed according to the manufacturers' instructions.

In the aesthetic zone, the implant head should be a minimum of 3 mm apical to an imaginary line connecting the cementoenamel junctions of the adjacent teeth and apical to the interproximal and crestal bone. A healing abutment or cover screw is placed in the implant. The healing abutment should be even with or slightly apical to the adjacent marginal tissues. Interproximal papillae adjacent to the implant can be adapted with interrupted sutures under minimal tension. The provisional restoration which should have an ovate pontic is then inserted, and evaluated, making certain that it is clear of the healing abutment to support the adjacent tissues and help preserve soft tissue anatomy adjacent to the implant. The patient is instructed after surgery care and sutures are removed in 7 to 10 days. Restoration of the implant can take place once osseointegration has been confirmed (maxillary anterior region four to six months). In the event that an immediately placed implant would encroach upon the maxillary sinus, it might be prudent to delay implant placement, augment the sinus, allow for bone healing and then place the implant.

The Gap

The marginal tissues do not adapt to the healing abutment. If the gap is too wide, connective tissue forms between the coronal implant aspect and surrounding bone. A series of animal 17 and human studies have demonstrated that small gaps between implants and bone will fill with bone with or without grafting materials or barriers.

Special implants were inserted into the defects, leaving a 1.0-2.5 mm gap between the implants and surrounding bone. Bovine bone alone or with a resorbable barrier was used to augment some sites, while others were left to spontaneously heal. It was demonstrated that at four months, all defects filled with newly formed bone and the biomaterial placed in the marginal defect in conjunction with implant became incorporated in newly formed bone tissue. A high degree of contact was established between the bovine bone particles and the newly formed bone (bovine bone did not enhance the process of bone formation and defect closure).

A prospective trial was conducted using various augmentation techniques at immediate implant sites. The efficacy of combinations of membranes and autogenous bone grafts at immediate implants were compared. Sixty-two consecutively treated patients each received an immediate implant for a single tooth replacement at a maxillary anterior or premolar site. Dimensions of the peri-implant defect at the implant collar were measured as follows:

Vertical defect height (VDH), horizontal defect depth (HDD) and horizontal defect width (HDW). Each implant randomly received one of five augmentation treatments and was submerged with connective tissue grafts:

Group 1 expanded polytetrafluoroethylene membrane only, Group 2 resorbable polylactide/polyglycolide copolymer membrane only, Group 3 resorbable membrane and autogenous bone graft; Group 4 autogenous bone graft only, and Group 5 no membrane and no bone graft control.

Comparisons between groups showed no significant differences for VDH (mean 75.4%) and HDD (mean 77%) reduction, differences were observed between groups for HDW reduction (range, 34.1-67.3%), with membrane-treated Groups 1, 2 and 3 showing the greatest reduction. In the presence of dehiscence defects of the labial plate, HDW reduction of 66.6% was achieved with membrane use compared with 37.7% without membranes. Over 50% more labial plate resorption occurred in the presence of a dehiscence defect irrespective of the augmentation treatment used. The results indicate that VDH and HDD reduction at defects adjacent to immediate implants may be achieved without the use of membranes and/or bone grafts.

In practice, when the gap is present no effort is made to surgically advance the flap. A small amount of allograft or alloplast is layered between the margin and implant abutment. This material is left exposed. Within a few weeks, some of it will be exfoliated and gingival mucosa will migrate over the exposed materials and healing is uneventful. Bovine bone has been used to augment small gaps adjacent to immediately placed implants, but results demonstrate that it does not affect their survival. Placement of such substances with or without barrier membranes may support or improve soft tissue contours; however, these materials cannot be relied upon to enhance osseointegration.

Socket preservation:

Socket preservation implies the placement of varying implantable materials within the sockets alone or with barrier membranes that maintain socket anatomy. Placement of foreign materials into extraction sockets will interfere with normal bone formation.

Iasella et al. compared normal socket healing with those grafted with demineralised freeze-dried bone and covered with a collagen barrier membrane. Unaugmented or grafted sockets decreased in width by an average of 1.7 mm, while grafted sites decreased by 1.2 mm (difference of 0.5 mm). The quantity of bone observed on histologic analysis was slightly greater in preservation sites, although these sites included both vital and non-vital bone. Other studies compared ridge dimensions and histologic characteristics of ridges preserved with two different graft materials. Twenty-four subjects, each requiring a non-molar extraction and delayed implant placement, were randomly selected to receive ridge preservation treatment with either an allograft in an experimental putty carrier plus a calcium sulphate barrier or a bovine-derived xenograft plus a collagen membrane. Horizontal and vertical ridge dimensions were determined using a digital calliper and a template. At four months postextraction, a trephine core was obtained for histologic analysis. Allograft mixed with an experimental putty carrier produced significantly more vital bone fill than did the use of a xenograft with no carrier material. Ridge width and height dimensions were similarly preserved with both graft materials. Placement of materials into extraction sockets might be termed osseointerference. Resorbable barriers without grafting reduce alveolar ridge resorption after tooth extraction.

Following the elevation of buccal and lingual full-thickness flaps and extraction of teeth, experimental sites were covered with bioabsorbable membranes; control sites did not receive barrier membranes. Titanium pins served as fixed reference 19 points for measurements. Flaps were advanced in order to achieve primary closure of the surgical wound. There was no membrane exposure during the course of healing. Reentry surgeries were performed at six months. Results showed that experimental sites presented with significantly less loss of alveolar bone height, more internal socket bone fill, and less horizontal resorption of the alveolar bone ridge. This study suggests that treatment of extraction sockets with membranes made of glycolide and lactide polymers is valuable in preserving alveolar bone in extraction sockets and preventing alveolar ridge defects. Placement of implants into these materials may limit osseointegration.

FIVE

IMPRESSION TECHNIQUES FOR IMPLANT DENTISTRY

The object of making an impression in implant dentistry is to accurately relate an analogue of the implant or implant abutment to the other structures in the dental arch.

For implant impressions, addition silicones (or poly-vinyl-siloxane) and polyether are currently considered as the materials of choice. Comparative studies have been published, investigating the accuracy and clinical behaviour of both elastomeric impression materials. Most researchers agree that there is no significant difference in the accuracy of implant impression between poly-vinyl-siloxane and polyether. Furthermore, Wenz, et al, compared the different impression techniques using only addition silicone and concluded that the single-step technique resulted in more accurate impressions. Regarding the viscosity of the impression material, the use of medium viscosity offers certain advantages in clinical practice. Medium viscosity or monophase materials can flow around the impression posts without exerting pressure. Due to their increased hardness after polymerization, an accurate impression can be achieved. Their use however should be combined with a custom tray that allows an even thickness of the impression material around the implants. Medium viscosity materials can be used alone or combined with high flowing materials to achieve maximum detail reproduction or to allow the material to flow/penetrate even in small gaps around the impression posts. Putty or high viscosity impression materials offer rigidity and can also be used but their flow is limited compared to medium viscosity. For this reason, putty or low flowing (high viscosity) materials should be used in combination with high flowing (low viscosity) flowing materials to achieve detail reproduction.

The choice of the impression technique and the accuracy of the resulting impression relates directly to the passive fit of the implant-supported restoration, which is an important goal in 20 the restorative procedure. An inaccurate impression may result in a metal framework fitting non-passively, which can cause mechanical complications such as screw loosening or fracture, and/or abutment fracture. The most commonly used and widely adopted impression techniques for implants in clinical practice are the open tray technique and the closed tray technique.

This is affected by the use of impression coping, which is incorporated into an impression.

Impression coping has two general forms, one type is retained in the mouth when the set impression is removed – this is known as the transfer type impression coping. The other type is incorporated in the impression and is removed from the mouth together with the set impression and is known as a pickup type impression coping. Characteristics of the transfer type impression coping are that they remain in the mouth on the removal of the set impression, the analogue is attached to the impression coping after removal from the mouth and this assembly is replaced in the indentation left on the set impression. No custom tray is required for this type of impression.

Characteristics of the pick up type impression coping are that they are removed from the mouth together with the set impression. They require access to the retaining screw to allow the release prior to removal of the impression coping — impression assembly, the analogues are attached to the impression copings while they are embedded in the impression tray. A custom tray with access to the impression coping screws is required.

When there is a limited mouth opening the transfer type impression coping can be used as there may not be sufficient space for access to the screws retaining pick up type impression copings with the impression in place and in patients with an exaggerated gag reflex, when the impression has to be removed as quickly as possible. The fidelity of the impression with respect to dimensional stability is critical; small discrepancies can lead to difficulty when the restoration is fabricated and delivered.

When impressions are required for multi implant restorations the precision of the impression is even more critical. This is because frameworks will be constructed from the master cast and misfit can lead to the stress applied to the implants on screwing down the framework. Bone loss and even loss of integration have been attributed to this misfit. Use an open custom tray that is rigid, to allow access to the retaining screws of pick up impression copings, to use a polyvinyl siloxane. Methods are available to capture this information on the master cast and they are as follows:

1. Fabricating a custom impression coping which is adapted to the soft tissue contours
2. Replacing the provisional restoration on the master cast and forming the soft tissue around the submucosal areas of the provisional restoration
3. Incorporating the provisional restoration into the impression.

Customised impression copings that accurately record the soft tissue can be made by attaching an analogue and placing some impression material around the submucosal portion of the provisional restoration, which on setting can be returned to the patient. A soft tissue cast is poured around the customised impression coping producing a cast with the implant position and soft tissue representing the intraoral conditions. When screw-retained restorations are used, the provisional restoration itself can be used as a pickup type impression coping. A soft tissue cast is poured around the exposed provisional after a coping is attached, yielding a soft tissue cast that is identical to that seen intraorally. This allows communication of some vital information to the technician fabricating the definitive restorations.

Various situations using different types of tray techniques are as follows:

1. Closed Tray Technique, Single Implant

In cases of single implants that have adequate distance to the adjacent teeth and favourable inclination, both the open tray and the closed tray technique can be applied. A-silicones can be used in putty consistency combined with low viscosity flowing material and prefabricated metal tray, as used for natural teeth(Fig 1-3). Also, impression posts with a plastic transfer cup that facilitates the repositioning of the post in the mass of polymerized impression material to minimize inaccuracy can be used. A medium viscosity material combined with low viscosity has been used. The patient was restored with a screw-retained implant-supported crown(Fig 4).

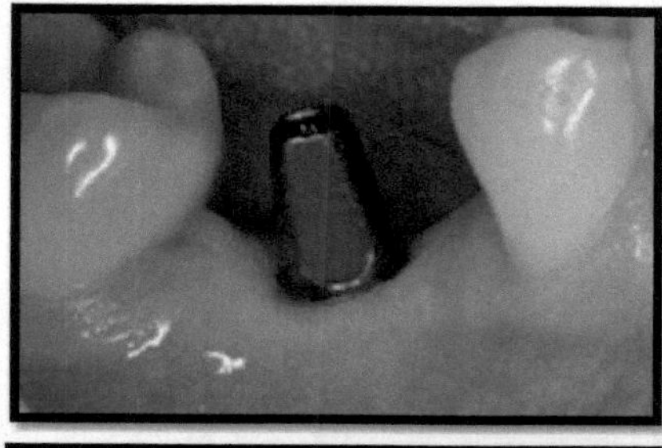

Fig 1: Abutment in position

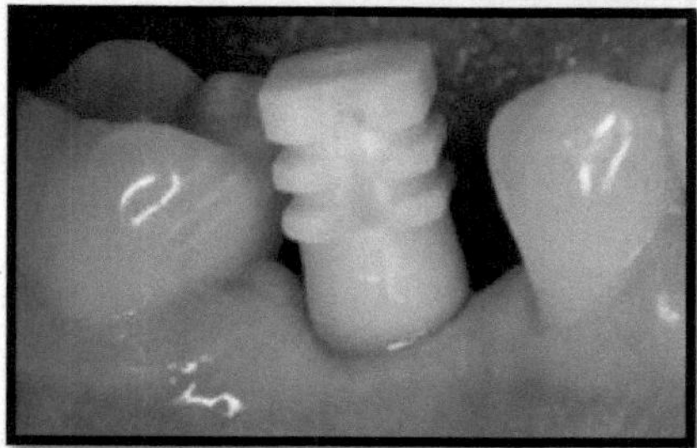

Fig 2: Plastic transfer caps fitted on the abutment

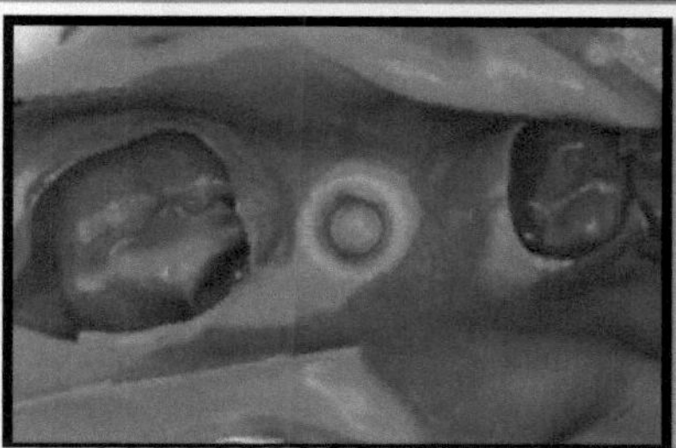

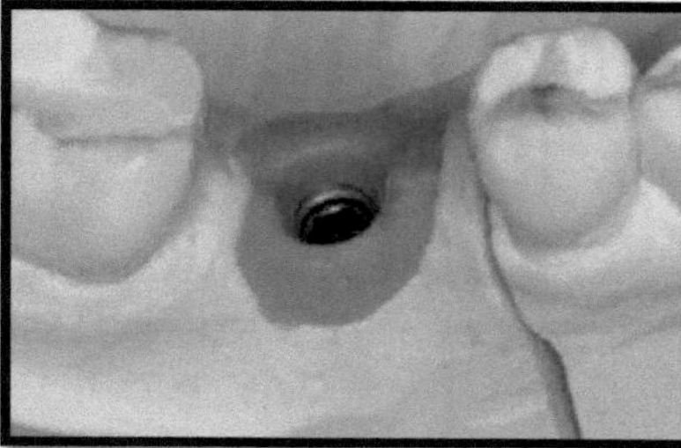

Fig 3a: Closed tray impression

Fig 3b: The working cast

2. Closed Tray Technique, Two Implants

In the presented case two mandibular right side implants (regions # 44 and 46) were to be restored. As the position and the inclination of the implants were favourable and the distance to the adjacent tooth adequate, the closed-tray technique (repositioning technique) was applied. On the impression posts, the plastic caps for the repositioning were fitted. An addition silicone was used in heavy and light consistency with a prefabricated metal tray and an accurate working cast was fabricated (Fig 6). The implant was restored with an implant-supported screw-retained fixed dental prosthesis (FDP) that fitted accurately.

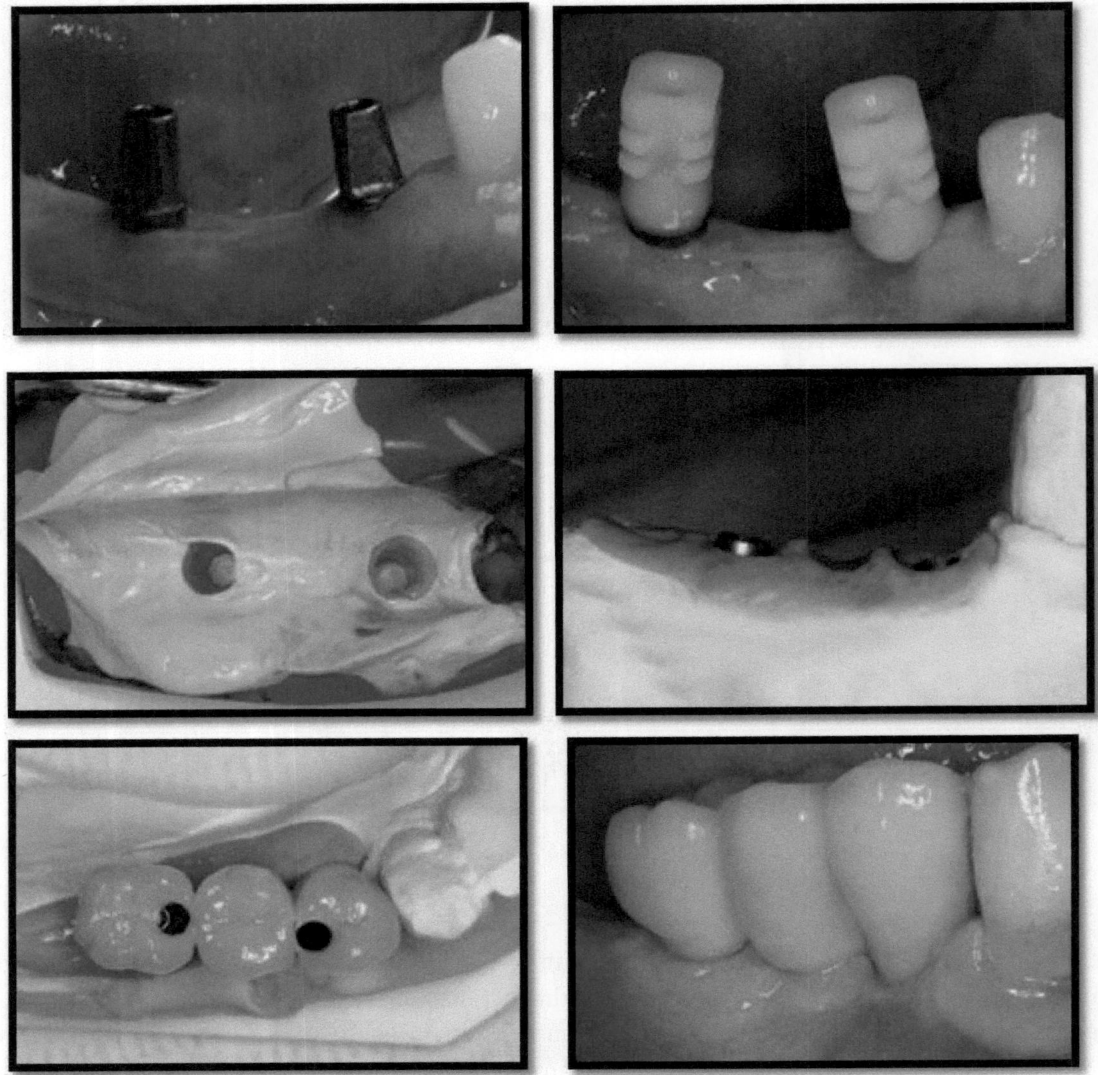

Fig 5a: Abutments in position Fig 5b: Plastic transfer caps for repositioning fitted on the abutmentsFig 6a: Closed tray impression Fig 6b: Working cast Fig 7a: Screw retained restoration Fig 7b: Intraoral view of the restoration

3. Open Tray Technique, Partially Edentulous Patient

In case B two adjacent implants in the maxillary right region (# 15,16) had to be restored and also the tooth # 14 with a crown. Due to the proximity and the unfavourable inclination of the implants, the open tray technique was selected. The thickness of the peri-implant tissues would also increase the difficulty for proper insertion of the transfer caps on the impression. A custom tray from the light-curing resin was fabricated on a study cast made from an initial impression with alginate. The height of the tray was checked to verify access to the impression posts. An additional type of silicone was used in medium and light viscosity both for the implants and the tooth and an accurate working cast could be fabricated. The use of medium and low viscosity silicone was advantageous in this case as the space between the implants was narrow and a heavy or putty material could not embrace the impression posts. The patient was restored with two splinted screw-retained crowns on the implants and a metal-ceramic crown on the tooth.

4. Open Tray Technique, Partially Edentulous Patient

Three adjacent implants were to be restored in the mandibular left side in regions # 34,35,36. The implants were not parallel with unfavourable inclinations. Additionally, the anterior implant was placed deep subgingivally and for these reasons, the open tray technique was selected. As the patient was on a heavy schedule and it was not possible to make a custom tray in the dental laboratory, a prefabricated plastic tray was used modified with openings for the impression posts. In order to achieve maximum accuracy of the impression, the impression posts were splinted with auto polymerizing resin which was added on a scaffold created with dental floss around and between the implants. An additional type of silicone was used. The medium viscosity of the material allowed the flow under the splinting and the increased hardness after polymerization contributed to the secure removing of the splinted impression posts in the material. An accurate working cast was fabricated and the patient was restored with splinted screw-retained crowns.

5. Open Tray Technique without Splinting, Edentulous Maxilla

Four implants were inserted in the edentulous maxilla according to the short dental arch principle. The implants were parallel with a favourable inclination with exception of the implant # 23 that had a severely divergent axis. As the distance between the implants was adequate, it was decided to take the impression with the open tray technique without splinting the impression posts. A custom tray was fabricated on a study cast in the dental laboratory using light-polymerizing resin. The tray was tried on the patient with the impression posts fixed on the implants to verify an undisturbed insertion path. It is important to verify the correct path of insertion before loading the impression material as the tray may need modification to allow proper placement. The impression was taken using medium viscosity material. The patient was restored with an implant-retained fixed restoration.

6. Open Tray Technique with Splinting, Edentulous Mandible

Four implants were inserted in the anterior region of the mandible for hybrid screw-retained fixed restoration according to the short dental arch principle. For the open tray technique, a custom tray was fabricated on a study cast without a handle in the anterior region that would cause difficulties to remove the retaining screws of the post. The impression posts for the open tray in this implant system were shorter and their embedment and retention in the impression material was doubtful. The posts were splinted by means of dental floss forming a scaffold on which auto polymerizing resin was added to create a block. The impression was taken using medium viscosity addition silicone both under the impression posts and in the tray. The patient was restored with a screw-retained hybrid restoration

7. Open Tray Technique with Splinting in Severely Reduced Space, Adjacent Implants

In this case, two adjacent implants were placed in the maxillary left region for the replacement of teeth 24 and 25. The implants were in proximity and it was not possible to insert the impression posts simultaneously. The possible clinical options for this case were either the modification of the posts by grinding the opposing sides or the impression of each implant separately. Instead of using the impression posts, the implant carriers were fitted on the implants and were used as impression posts. The carriers have the same diameter as the implants (narrower than impression posts) and fit exactly to the internal hexagon to the interior of the implant. The main problem of using the carriers as impression posts is that due to their design the repositioning in the impression material is not accurate. Additionally, the carriers are provided with short screws and cannot be used as impression posts for the open tray technique. Taking into consideration the above-mentioned limitations, it was decided to use the carriers with an open custom tray by splinting. The carriers were fixed on the implants and were splinted using auto polymerizing resin covering the whole edentulous space. Before taking the impression the unobstructed removal of the block of resin was checked. The impression was taken using heavy body addition silicone for the tray that had the proper stiffness to engage the block and remove it. Low viscosity silicone was injected under the block for the reproduction of details. Alternatively, medium viscosity combined with low viscosity material could also have been used. This impression technique resulted in a working cast with the needed precision and detail that allowed the construction of two splinted screw-retained crowns fitting accurately.

SIX

1. ESTHETICS

When the implant is placed in the ideal position, predictable esthetics can be realized with either a screw- or a cement-retained prosthesis. In situations, where the implant is placed in a position that will cause the screw access to emerge in the esthetic zone, a cement-retained restoration is a preferred method. The abutment of cement-retained restorations can be prepared in the same way as in natural teeth and the crown can then be cemented. All ceramic screw-retained crowns reduce the challenge of masking underlying discolouration from showing through the occlusal access opening once it is sealed by resin cement. Screwretained restorations have been criticized because the access hole will exit through the central fossa of the prosthetic crown. It may compromise esthetic, occlusion, and porcelain strength; especially if the diameter of the screw is wide. The cemented crown has no entrance cavity. To overcome these problems, pre-angled/angled/customed abutments have been used so that the screw access opening is relocated to the cingulum or occlusal surface. However, the screw must diverge at least 17 degrees from the long axis of the implant to allow sufficient space for the retention screw. Even in the posterior area, the occlusal restoration may still compromise the esthetics because of the underlying dark metal oxide. When there is difficulty in placing the implant in an ideal position for any anatomic limitation, the pre-angled or custom abutments can be used so that the screw access channel is relocated away from the esthetic area. The use of an opaquer in combination with resilient composite offers a significant esthetic improvement of the implant restoration. With adequate treatment planning and the use of surgical guides, the implants should be placed in the ideal position, allowing the dentist the choice of either screw- or cement-retained restorations.

In screw-retained restorations, the implants are placed palatally in the anterior region of the maxilla to allow screw emergence through the cingulum area. Palatal implant placement results in a porcelain ridge lap, which compromises hygiene. Also, restoration is cantilevered facially from the implant body, which results in offset loading of the implant. In the posterior region, the access hole exits through the central fossa of the prosthetic tooth. This is not only a cosmetic compromise but also an occlusal one. The esthetic outcome of the cement-retained prosthesis is more favourable than the screw-retained prosthesis.

There are situations where screw retention is not possible due to implant position, in these situations having screw access in a visible area is unacceptable.

Aesthetics is dependent largely on patient selection, tissue volume, tissue type surrounding the implant and implant position. The trajectory of the implant will merely determine the method of retention. Cement retention can be used more universally and screw-retained restorations can only be used when the trajectory of the implant allows the screw access to be in non-aesthetic areas.

2. RETRIEVABILITY

A major advantage of the use of screw-retained restorations is that they allow the retrieval of the restoration without damage to the restoration or fixture. Therefore, the screws and restorations can be re-torqued, fractured components can be repaired, implant and soft tissue can be evaluated, calculus can be removed, and cleaning of the components is possible. The retrievability may be most valuable in extensive cases, where the prosthesis needs to be retrieved for maintenance purposes.

The technique used to remove a screw-retained prosthesis involves removal of the occlusal restoration, the intermediate cotton pellet, and the coping screw. When the restoration is removed, it can be screwed back in subsequently. A new cotton pellet is placed and the access hole is then restored with materials such as composites.

Retrievability in cement-retained restorations is possible with the use of soft access cement as a luting agent. Cement does not adhere as tenaciously to implant abutments as they are smooth and well-polished without any undercuts when compared to their natural counterparts. In case frequent debonding with soft access cement is seen, even harder cement can be used and yet still be removed readily. However, harder cement when removed results in scratches on implant abutment. This could act as the site for plaque accumulation. Hence, implant components of alloys with improved mechanical properties are preferred.

A temporary cement composed of zinc oxide-eugenol or mixed with petroleum jelly is frequently used as a final cement for implant crowns to allow for future retrieval.

Another technique used to retrieve a cement-retained crown was described using set screws. The idea is to place a retrieval screw in an area where the cement seal can be broken without damaging the restoration. Other techniques involve the use of guides to reach the screw underneath or the use of screws to move the abutments and then retrieve the restoration. If the abutment becomes loose, if the restoration requires a repair and cannot be uncemented, or if the crown cannot be salvaged then fabrication of a new crown is suggested. As a consequence, the additional cost is charged to the patient.

One of the techniques described is the incorporation of screws into the cemented restoration to be used later to lift the restoration off the abutment if activated. Compared with conventional screw retention, this technique improves esthetics and occlusion since the access hole can be placed in the most ideal position without regard to the implant position.

Another method is to prepare a cylindrical guide hole on the lingual surface of the abutment and an access hole on the lingual side of the restoration. Then, by inserting a removing driver into the guide hole through the access hole and turning it to generate a shear force, the cement will disintegrate and, the restoration can be easily removed.

Other techniques that have been suggested depend mainly on locating the screw access opening of the abutment screw that is achieved by using an abutment screw access guide or placement of a well-defined small ceramic stain on the occlusal surface of restoration where the screw access opening is located. Combining both screws- and cement-retained restorations in the same prosthesis were introduced by using at least 1 screw retainer into a series of cement retainers within the same prosthesis.

Using abutment inserts is a technique developed so that there will be no need for either screw or cement for connecting the restoration to the abutment. In this technique, a standard abutment with perforation on the lingual side is screwed to the implant. An insert is cast to fit tightly into the abutment in a lock and key fashion, and the same insert lodges into the screw of the implant to secure it. This insert has a perforation to match the lingual perforation of the abutment. Then, the restoration is made with a lingual hole to match the abutment and insert 38 through a spring-locked pin. An explorer can be used to push the spring to release the crown for removal. Provisional cement is frequently used as final cement for cement-retained implant-supported restorations to allow for future retrieval. In spite of all the proposed techniques to improve the retrievability in the cement-retained prosthesis, screw retention becomes more necessary in extensive cases where prosthesis needs more maintenance, so cantilevered prostheses and full-arch implant reconstruction are best restored with screw retention.

3. PASSIVITY

Passive casting is one of the important prerequisites for the long-term success of implant prostheses to prevent biological and prosthetic complications. The former includes increased transfer of load to the bone resulting in bone loss, and development of microflora at the gap between the implant and abutment. The latter includes loosening or fracture of the fastening screw, implant fracture and unretained restorations. Truly passive screw-retained implant prosthesis is virtually impossible to fabricate. The passive fit was described by Branemark to be ideally in the 10 μm range. However, this is not attainable in screw-retained prosthesis due to dimensional discrepancies inherent in the clinical and laboratory procedures which include, distortion when final impression material shrinks while setting, dental stone expansion, wax pattern distortion while setting or spruing, expansion of investment material, shrinkage of metal casting, acrylic/porcelain shrinkage, soldering inaccuracies, and manufacturer variance of a number of the implant component.

However, the passivity of casting is not an issue in cement-retained prostheses. The absence of a screw connecting the superstructure to the abutment or to the implant tends to eliminate the strain that is introduced into the prosthesis/implant system during the tightening of this screw. In this attachment system, die spacers create 40 µm of cement space that compensates for the dimensional variations of laboratory materials and permits the fabrication of a more passive casting with cement-retained restorations. Further, if the casting is not passive, the abutment may be modified slightly at the same try-in appointment. The resolution of the same difficulty in screw-retained prosthesis requires separation and soldering of the casting or altogether new fabrication of casting.

There are methods of fabricating and making frameworks more passive such as EDM (Electric Discharge Machining) or directly luting the framework to abutments seated onto 39 implants intra-orally with composite resin. These techniques can be used with screw-retained prostheses. To eliminate errors from casting and shrinkage of metal, several implant manufacturers are machining titanium frameworks to fit implant analogues on master casts. While this has potential at present, frameworks are not well designed and clinicians are limited to using all components from specific companies. As this technology improves designs will improve and the process will be less restrictive with respect to implants and components used. EDM and milled titanium frameworks only address the errors of casting; and not the errors of impression making and distortion of the master cast.

Distortion of the impression material, setting expansion of the dental stone, wax pattern and metal casting shrinkage are all contributing factors to the non-passive fitting of the framework. There can be two possible complications of non-passive fitting of the frameworks:

A. Biological complications: Increased transfer of load to the bone, bone loss, and development of microflora at the gap between the implant and the abutment.

B. Prosthetic complications: Loosening or fracture of the fastening screw.

Fulcrums or pivot points are created at the edge where the abutment meets the head of the implant. The torque that is applied to tighten the screw in the screw-retained implant prosthesis is converted into tensile force (preload Fs x r). The upsetting masticatory Occlusal force (Fo), can be resolved into its component: vertical (Fv) and horizontal forces (Fh). To maintain equilibrium, the resisting moment of the screw (Fs x r) must be greater than or equal to the sum of the moments created by the offset loading (F v x L2 + F h x L1) (Fig. 1). If there is an accurate fit between the head of the implant and abutment, a continuum of pivot points is created around the circumference. In this stable situation, the vertical occlusal force will not stress the screw or cause screw loosening. However, when inaccurate castings are screwed into implants, gaps are created and vertical loading over the implant head can compress the casting and cause screw loosening. In this situation, the load is applied outside the pivot point (offset loading) and a sufficient magnitude has to overcome the clamping force of the screw.

4. ACCESSIBILITY

Placing a screw-retained restoration in a patient with a limited opening and/or in the posterior area of the mouth can be challenging if there was not sufficient space for the screw-driver to 40 be inserted. The implant-abutment connection must line up with the interproximal contacts to allow seating for the one-piece restoration. In addition to the difficulty of access, the use of screw-retained restorations in the posterior part of the mouth may carry a risk of swallowing or aspirating the screw or screwdriver. A cement-retained crown may be easier to deliver in these situations. They offer easier access to the posterior of the mouth, especially in patients with limited jaw opening.

5. IMPLANT INCLINATION

When the screw-retained crown is planned to be the prosthetic choice, the dentist should bring to attention the inclination of the implant fixture accordingly while planning the surgical procedure. This does not cause a problem with posterior implants, since they are more axially positioned with regard to the alveolus and tooth. However, it may be an issue with anterior teeth where the implant needs to be inclined lingually to allow screw emergence through the cingulum area of the restoration.

6. HYGIENE

Excess cement left behind cemented restoration is a major problem and can result in soft tissue damage, bone loss, and/or chronic inflammation. The soft tissue surrounding screw-retained crowns are healthier than the peri-implant mucosa surrounding cemented restorations. By removing cement thoroughly, the risk of peri-implantitis is reduced significantly.

Screw-retained restorations that have openings, placed facially are planned in a more palatal direction so that the access hole to the prosthetic screw is placed in the cingulum area. Hence, a facial porcelain ridge lap is required to achieve a proper emergence profile. This makes the cervical sulcus of the implant inaccessible for hygiene. However, this is not seen with cement-retained restorations, because the implant may be placed under the incisal edge, rather than the cingulum.

7. AXIAL LOADING

Axial loading of the implant is important for proper load distribution. To achieve this, primary occlusal contacts are placed on the implant head. However, this is not feasible with a screw-retained prosthesis because of screws and overlying occlusal obturation material, which are not capable of taking axial loading. Therefore, the primary occlusal contact is often placed on the buccal cusp in the mandible that creates an offset load. According to various biomechanical principles, increased offset loads increases the stress at the bony interface resulting in an increased incidence of screw loosening and breakage. In cemented prosthesis, the primary occlusal contact is directly over the top of each implant and has the ability to vertically load the prosthetic head of the implant.

8. OCCLUSION

Screw holes in the occlusal surfaces of teeth provide poor esthetics and disrupt the occlusal surfaces. The establishment of ideal occlusal contacts in screw-retained prostheses may not be possible, because the access hole occupies a significant portion of the occlusal table. As the size of the implant increases so is the screw access hole, thus leading to a large occlusal restoration, which may compromise the long-term durability. The screw access hole occupies about 50% of the occlusal table in molars and 75% in premolars. They interfere with centric occlusal contacts and also affect protrusive and lateral excursive movements. To establish proper occlusal contacts, this should be done on composite material. However, these contacts will not be stable long term, because, composite material wears, especially when the opposing restorative material is porcelain. This occlusal discrepancy can be overcome with the use of a TS (Transversal) screw; that fixes the prosthesis to the abutment, but it is necessary to have good oral access in the palatal or lingual area.

With cement-retained prostheses, ideal and stable occlusal contacts can be established and remain stable over a long period of time. Because there is no access hole on the occlusal surface, an axial load may be directed to the implant, which is preferable to lateral forces. Hence, the occlusal function is promoted with a cement-retained prosthesis.

9. EASE OF FABRICATION AND COST

The fabrication of cement-retained prostheses is easier than that for screw-retained prostheses because traditional prosthetic techniques are followed and there is no need for special training of the laboratory technicians. As manufacturers do not provide pre-angled abutments for screw-type restorations with the divergence of the screw path of less than 17°, restoration of implants is easier with cement-retained prostheses. Provisional crowns are easier to fabricate with cement-retained prostheses than screw-retained ones.

The screw-retained restorations are usually 1.5 to 2 times more expensive because of the extra time and components needed, such as plastic sleeves, laboratory fixation screws, and the analogues themselves.

The increased cost of the screw-retained restoration that allows for predictable retrievability must not be compared to the potential costs of damaging the cemented restoration if a biological or technical complication occurs.

SEVEN

SOME SITUATIONS PREFER ONE METHOD OF RETENTION OVER THE OTHER

The selection of an implant system is the first step in determining the feasibility of either a cement or screw retention for the prosthesis. The current implant systems that employ a conical interface between the implant and the abutment or other internally designed connection features have reduced the incidence of screw loosening and other problems associated with traditional hex-top systems. Therefore, it is much easier and simpler to utilize the traditional cementation procedures with these current systems for retaining definitive prostheses. However, there are some situations where it is better or more suitable to use one method of retention rather than another. These situations are:

Those that favour screw retention –

- Large, full-arch implant reconstructions are preferred to be screw-retained because complications in long-span prostheses are more common than in short-span ones.
- Cantilevered prostheses are preferred to be screw-retained because some maintenance of restorative structures or implants would be needed during the lifetime of such prostheses.
- With patients who are at a high risk of developing gingival recession, screw-retained restorations are preferred. This allows their uncomplicated removal and then the modification of the restorations according to the new situation.
- With patients who are expected to lose more teeth in the future, screw-retained restorations are preferred. This is to allow for easy removal of the restorations, thereby modifying the restorations.
- In situations where minimal interocclusal space exists, it may not be possible to achieve adequate retention for cement-retained restorations because these restorations require a vertical component of at least 5 mm to provide retention and resistance form. However, as little as 4 mm of interocclusal space is sufficient to use screw-retained restorations. Additionally, screw-retained restorations can be attached directly to implants without an intermediate abutment, therapy reducing the interocclusal space needed for these restorations.
- In situations in which removal of excess cement is difficult or impossible (eg, if the final restorative margin will be greater than 3 mm subgingivally, the use of screw-retained restoration is indicated). An alternative to screw-retained restoration in this 44 situation would be to fabricate a custom abutment for cement retention with a restorative margin following the outline of the gingival contours.
- In cases in which technical or biological complications are anticipated, screw-retained restorations are preferred to allow for easy removal of the restorations, thereby managing the problems.

Those that favour cement retention –

- Single-unit and short-span implant restorations, assuming that implant table size, implant numbers, and abutment screw torque can be optimized, are preferred to be cement-retained. The only reason for using screw retention in such cases would be if the implant's long axis is too palatal in the anterior region.
- Cases involving narrow diameter crowns in which the screw access may compromise the crown's integrity are preferred to be cement-retained.
- Situations in which the occlusal surface will be compromised with regard to esthetics or occlusal stability due to the presence of a restorative material sealing the screw access are preferred to be cement-retained.
- In situations of restoring malaligned implants, if the divergence of the implant axis and the retaining screw of the angled abutment which is to receive the restoration is less than 17°, conventional screw retention of the restoration using pre-machined abutments is not possible.

Ideally, implants should be placed parallel to one another and be aligned vertically with axial forces. However, anatomical constraints can sometimes prevent the clinician from placing implants at ideal angulations to allow for a screw-retained prosthesis. Historically, restoring with a cemented restoration, performing surgical correction (for example, bone grafting) or relocating the implant position/trajectory used to be the only options. Several prosthetic components have been introduced that can compensate for and redirect the angulation of the prosthesis into a more favourable position to restore. pre-angled abutments, dynamic abutments, and ASCs are alternatives for cement-retained prostheses on unfavourably angulated implants.

PRE-ANGLED ABUTMENTS

Pre-angled abutments can redirect screw access openings to the occlusal or cingulum areas of implant restorations through the use of two off-axis screws: one screw to secure the abutment into the implant and the second screw at an angle to secure the crown into the bulk of the abutment structure. However, to provide a sufficient abutment structure to house a retention screw for the restoration, the long axis of the implant and path of the retention screw must diverge significantly. At a minimum, Nobel Biocare provides a screw-retained pre-angled abutment with a divergence of 17°. A 30° component is also available for more severely angled implants.

Some research suggests that off-axis loading induces excessive lateral stress onto the supporting implants, supporting bone, and prosthesis which could trigger complications. While this concept is true, Clelland et al. and Celletti et al. found that the principal strains were considered to be within the physiologic zone for bone and the restorative materials. Goodacre et al. found a higher proportion of abutment screw loosening in angled abutments; however, the screws were reported to be titanium. The incidence of screw loosening dropped considerably once they were replaced with gold abutment screws (which can produce higher preloads when torqued). It is suggested that occlusion is minimized on inclines of the restoration, and if possible, avoid lateral excursions on teeth with pre-angled abutments. Clinical significance There is a general consensus that pre-angled screw-retained abutments produce no additional clinically evident physiological disadvantages over traditional abutments. From a biomechanical point of view, the pre-angled abutment may be a suitable restorative option for implants with a nonideal angulation.

DYNAMIC ABUTMENTS

In 2004, the dynamic abutment, a biomechanically novel abutment design was introduced. This allows for 360° variability in abutment angulation up to 28° off-axis. Unlike the pre-angled abutment which has thick labial margins and requires more apical placement to hide the components, the benefit here is that the labial dimensions are quite thin so implant placement does not have to occur further apically. The abutment consists of a base with an occlusal semi-sphere, on which sits a burnout chimney that has 28° of rotation freedom. The angle is chosen and set prior to casting the abutment. Once fabricated, the abutment is secured using a screw with a uniquely fluted screw head and a screwdriver containing a sphere head with 1.3 mm hexagonal facets. Research from the Herman Ostrow School of Dentistry by Lee et al. showed that deviation of the restoration from the implant axis did not have any significant influence on the screw removal torque values and fracture resistance of the screw after 5 years of simulated loading compared to a standard 3i Biomet gold screw. Dynamic abutments may be the preferred option over pre-angled abutments as the components are thinner and less intrusive on the peri-implant tissues. A custom angle can be selected anywhere from 0° to 28°.

ANGULATED SCREW CHANNEL

Most recently, Nobel Biocare launched a variation on the dynamic abutment: The ASC abutment. This system offers a much simpler alternative to the cement-retained prosthesis in the restoration of tilted implants. The technician can "bend" the screw access channel into a more favourable position up to 25° with 360° of variability. The abutment is secured using an Omnigrip driver with rounded facets to engage the screw head. The head itself has multi-fluted reliefs cut into the walls to provide space for maximum angulation of the driver. With this design, torque can be applied consistently between 0° and 25° of angulation. Its use appears extremely promising, but additional research should be performed first to assess complication rates.

EIGHT

SCREW RETAINED CROWN RESTORATIONS OF SINGLE IMPLANTS

The two main procedures needed for getting a crown restoration are taking an accurate impression and delivering the screw-retained single crown. The prosthetic procedures are usually conducted after proper healing time is allowed following the surgical insertion of the implant. If surgical insertion followed a two-stage protocol, then a healing time of at least 2 weeks should be allowed after surgical exposure.

Various shapes and sizes of healing caps are available for different implant systems. Radiographic evaluation of the implant may be prescribed to evaluate the quality of bone surrounding the implant; an intraoral periapical X-ray can be used to check for any unwanted signs of a failure of the implant.

The following steps are presented to illustrate the technique of open tray direct impression:

1. Healing the abutment removal: The peri-implant mucosa is allowed to heal for at least 10 days after surgical exposure. The healing abutment is unscrewed by anti-clock-wise rotation using a manual screwdriver. The implant prosthetic platform should be examined to be free of bone and soft tissue.

2. A fixture mount/pick-up coping should be used which is suitable for the open-tray impression technique, is placed on the implant body and tightened by manual clock-wise rotation of its inner screw. When the mount is below the level of the mucosa, an intra-oral radiograph should be done to ensure that the mount is properly seated on the implant.

3. A plastic stock tray or a custom made acrylic tray should be customized by cutting out a window over the area of the implant to allow clearance for the fixture mount. The impression tray should be assessed in the oral cavity to verify that the fixture mount and its screw protrudes through the tray. A light-bodied addition silicone impression material is syringed around the fixture mount. Meanwhile, the impression tray is loaded with heavy-bodied addition silicone impression material and seated directly in the mouth and exactly in its place. The excess impression material should be wiped off the screw of the fixture mount before it sets. Opening of the screw may be filled with wax or cotton to prevent impression material from being trapped into screw opening.

4. After the impression material sets, the mount is separated from the implant by un-screwing the long screw inside the mount. Then the impression tray is removed from the mouth with the fixture mount remaining secured in the impression. The impression material is verified to be completely adapted around the implant and mount. Then the healing abutment is placed back onto the implant to prevent soft tissue collapse till next visit when the restoration is to be delivered. An interim crown may be fabricated to promote biologically and esthetically appropriate soft tissue emergence for implants in the esthetic zone.

5. The analog is mated with the fixture mount/transfer by holding the analog in place while inserting the long screws through the access holes in the impression tray and tightened by the hand screwing.

6. The analog should be safely and precisely attached to the impression fixture mount. Caution to avoid the over-rotation of the mount is needed during screwing since any slight movement may cause distortion of the

impression

7. Impression with the fixture mount connected to the analog, bite registration, opposing impression, and shade of the restoration is sent to the dental laboratory

PROSTHODONTIC PERSPECTIVE TO ALL-ON-4 CONCEPT FOR DENTAL IMPLANTS

The term **All-on-4** refers to **"all"** teeth being supported "on four" dental implants, a surgical and technique prosthodontics procedure for total rehabilitation of the edentulous patient or for patients with badly broken down teeth, decayed teeth or compromised teeth due to gum disease. The concept was developed by Paulo Malo with straight and angled multi-unit abutments, to provide edentulous patients with an immediately loaded full-arch restoration with only four implants.

The general considerations are:

- To achieve primary implant stability (35 to 45 Ncm insertion torque).
- Indicated with a minimum bone width of 5mm and minimum bone height of 10mm from canine to canine in the maxilla and 8mm in the mandible.
- If angulation is 30o or more, the tilted implants can be splinted.
- For tilted posterior implants, the distal screw access holes should be located at the occlusal face of the first molar, the second premolar, or the first premolar

Implants in the maxilla are placed with two distal implants in the posterior region which are tilted anteriorly to the maxillary antrum while in the mandible implants are positioned anterior to the mental foramen. They should be inserted at an angulation of 30o -45o. The use of the All-on-4 ® surgical guide assists in ensuring the placement of the implants with correct positioning, angulation and emergence. The guide is placed into a 2mm osteotomy that is made in the midline position of the maxilla or mandible and the titanium band is contoured to follow the arc of the opposing arch. The vertical lines on the guide are used as a reference for 52 drilling at the correct angulation, which should not be greater than 45o. The other guides that can be used for implant placement are Template, Angulated pins and Denture.

Straight, 17o multiunit abutments and 30o angulated abutments with different collar heights are placed onto the implants. These are used to achieve the correct access allowing relative parallelism so that the rigid prosthesis can be seated passively.

If an implant is part of a multi implant-supported prosthesis, the spread of implants and stiffness of the prosthesis will reduce bending of the implant. The more distal position of the posterior implant and the resulting shorter cantilever may have a role in the reduction of stress values in the implant. When the distal cantilevers of FFP are excessive in length, deformation of the framework can result in fracture of the prosthetic screw, the acrylic resin teeth or even the framework itself.

The use of angled abutments on two tilted implants placed in a curved arch and with cross arch splinting might help decrease the stresses around the distal implants. The connection of implants may provide a safer transfer of load on each implant and so the placement in healed or fresh extraction bone sights may not influence implant survival when rehabilitating totally edentulous mandibles.

From a prosthetic perspective, the high success rate obtained with this protocol, including minimal bone loss even with multiple extractions and bone reduction followed by immediate function is believed to be a result of –

- Stable splinting of all four implants with the provisional immediately after surgery,
- Careful occlusal adjustment to provide bilateral occlusion in the canine and first premolar areas,
- Avoid occlusal contact toward the distal of the prosthesis and maximize the anteroposterior spread.

An Anteroposterior spread that minimizes the distal cantilevers and establishes well distributed four-point stability was probably contributary to both implant and prosthetic success.

Open tray multi-unit impression copings are placed onto the multi-unit abutments, which are then splinted with a low shrinkage auto polymerising resin (GC pattern resin) and wire bars. This ensures an accurate transfer without accidental displacement of the impression copings. An open tray impression is made with a rigid polyvinyl siloxane material (3M ESPE Imprint Putty) to capture the positions of the implants and the soft tissues.

The prosthetic phase includes:

Step 1 - Open tray impression made with wire and GC resin splinting for improved accuracy

Step 2 - Final impressions after integration is verified, being splinted with GC resin and metal.

Step 3 - All-Ceramic Zirconia bridges being designed with CAD/CAM technology

Step 4 - Use of CAD/CAM zirconia bridge or Titanium framework milled for crown cementation

Step 5 - Crowns luted to zirconia framework

Step 6 - Implant-supported zirconia bridge framework with individual crowns luted

Provisional all-acrylic resin prosthesis is then constructed and issued to the patient within a few hours or overnight. The provisional prosthesis is torqued to 15Ncm. The patient is reviewed after one week, at three weeks, three months and then annually.

At the three month appointment, fabrication of the definitive bridge may be started. The final restorative solution can be a:

1. CAD/CAM designed fixed prosthesis with Zirconia or Titanium framework. Individual crowns are cemented to the final bridge framework.

2. Fixed prosthesis with CAD/CAM designed Titanium or Zirconia framework with acrylic veneering.

3. Fixed prosthesis with cast metal and veneering porcelain.

4. Removable final prosthesis: e.g. milled bar overdenture, MK1 attachment overdenture

Occlusal scheme of implant-prosthetic superstructure basic requirements are

1. Establishment of stable jaw relationships with maximum intercuspal contacts that are bilaterally identical

2. Establishment of " freedom in centric" within the overall occlusal scheme

3. Elimination of any interference between the maximum intercuspal and retruded contact positions

4. Provision of harmonic, free mandibular movements with light tooth contacts during both lateral and protrusive manoeuvres

Occlusal scheme for immediate loading for All-on-Four concept

Avoid or minimize the length of the cantilever. Simultaneous bilateral point contacts on all teeth, excluding teeth distal to implant emergence. In lateral movements, group function or guidance with flat linear pathways and minimal vertical superimposition excluding teeth in cantilever. In protrusive movements, guidance is distributed on all anterior teeth including canines, with flat linear pathways and minimal vertical superimposition. Even if the implant-supported prosthesis is opposed to a removable full denture, in excursive movements avoid balancing contacts.

Occlusal scheme for All-on-Four definitive prosthesis

Simultaneous bilateral point contacts on canine and posterior teeth and grazing contacts on incisors. In lateral movements, canine guidance opposing natural dentition, group function opposing posterior implant-supported bridge with flat linear pathways and minimum vertical superimposition. If the implant-supported prosthesis is opposed to removal, complete denture or implant-supported overdenture or a distal extension cast partial denture to leave the most distal tooth slightly out of occlusion and in excursive movements seek one or more balancing contacts, planning greater anteroposterior space at the anterior teeth. The occlusal pattern should have relatively flat cusps i.e. the inclination of the cuspal planes should be less than the inclinations of the condylar path.

Advantages

- Angled posterior implants avoid anatomical structures
- Angled posterior implants allow longer implants anchored in the better quality bone
- Reduces posterior cantilever
- Eliminates bone grafts in the edentulous maxilla and mandible in the majority of cases
- High success rates
- Implants well-spaced, good biomechanics, easier to clean
- Immediate function and aesthetics
- The final restoration can be fixed or removable
- Reduced cost due to less number of implants and avoidance of grafting in the majority of cases.

Limitations

- Good general health and acceptable oral hygiene;
- Sufficient bone for 4 implants of at least 10mm in length; and
- Implants attain sufficient stability for immediate function.

Disadvantages

- Free hand arbitrary surgical placement of the implant is not always possible as implant placement is completely prosthetically driven.
- The length of the cantilever in the prosthesis cannot be extended beyond the limit.

- It is very technique sensitive and requires elaborate pre-surgical preparation such as CAD/CAM, surgical splint.

The length of the cantilever in the prosthesis cannot be extended beyond the limit

A study was conducted to evaluate the most accurate impression technique for "All on Four" restoration, comparing conventional and digital impressions.

For this study, patients edentulous in at least one arch, presenting with severe posterior mandibular or maxillary atrophy were randomly selected. All patients underwent full-arch immediate-load rehabilitations, which were fixed to a total of four implants (two axial and two tilted). Following implant placement, patients were grouped into two. Conventional pickup was carried out in the control group, and digital impressions were performed in the test group. Following prosthetic rehabilitation, patients underwent intraoral digital radiographs to check for the presence of voids at the bar-implant connection and to evaluate accuracy. Three-, 6-, and 12-month follow-up examinations were performed.

Results show that a total of 25 patients received immediately loaded "All-on-Four" prostheses (17 maxillary, 13 mandibular) supported by four implants (total 120 implants), of which five received both maxillary and mandibular prosthetic rehabilitation. The digital impression procedure required significantly less time than the conventional procedure.

Thus, the study concluded that it is possible to develop computer-aided design/computer-assisted manufacturing (CAD/CAM) cobalt-chromium full-arch rehabilitations with satisfactory accuracy using digital impression techniques.

ALL- ON – 6 CONCEPT

All 6 dental procedure is the best solution for patients with enough bone structure in the jaw. It is a variation of the All-on-4 technique based on the same concept but instead of four, it uses six implants that are placed in areas of the mouth with the highest bone volume. This treatment is designed for patients with enough bone structure and is an alternative to traditional dental implants because it maximises bone potential.

In many cases, bone grafting is often necessary prior to implantation of traditional dental implants but All on 6 uses only six implants to anchor your denture where the bone is the strongest. Therefore, when using the All on 6 technique, bone grafting is rarely required.

Some people may not be suitable for dental implants, it depends on their current oral health, and also adequate bone structure in their jaw is needed to support the implant.

There remain situations when screw retention is not possible due to implant position, implant trajectory, aesthetics or function.

Off-axis implant placement can sometimes be compensated with angled abutments that still allow screw retention. For these angled abutments to be used the angle compensation must be more than 17 degrees.

This is to allow sufficient divergence in the trajectory of the abutment screw to still allow housing for the retentive screw of the restoration. If the divergence of the implant axis and the retaining screw of the abutment to receive the restoration is less than 17 degrees, there remains insufficient bulk of the abutment to house the retaining screw of the restoration. In these situations, lingual set screws can be incorporated to retain restorations on, essentially, abutments designed for cement retention.

Abutments to receive cemented implant restorations can be largely classified as stock or custom abutments. Stock abutments are fabricated by manufacturers and the cement margin and profile of the abutment are either made to average dimensions or ignored entirely.

The ideal implant position to obtain an aesthetic outcome will be located 3 mm or more below the buccal mucosal margin. When there is any scallop this can lead to the margin being 5-6 mm sub-mucosal in the interproximal areas.

If the form of the margin conforms to the abutment margin, this deep margin leads to two clinical problems: maintaining the soft tissue profile while the restoration is removed, and cement removal after cementation.

The use of stock abutments should be used only when minimal scallop of the mucosal margins are present and cement margins can be kept within 2-3 mm of the cement margin or stock abutments with supra-mucosal margins to be modified, to adapt more closely to mucosal margins to facilitate cement removal.

Custom abutments are either waxed onto machined cylinders to form and cast or machined from titanium via a computer-aided design (3i Encode, Nobelbiocare Procera, Zimmer Dental, Atlantis Abutments), or copied from a waxed form (Nobelbiocare Procera). When custom abutments are designed with the support of the soft tissue and cement margin location in mind, most of the problems of cementation with stock abutments can be overcome.

The ideal abutment should be tooth coloured; this will allow ideal soft tissue colouration and the best opportunity for aesthetics, as all-ceramic restorations can be used. At present alumina or zirconia abutments are available. When the abutment retaining screw access and angle correction is done, the resulting abutments are often left with very thin sections. These abutments are at risk of fracture due to these dimensions. Moreover, porcelain fails with crack propagation, and tensional forces in a wet environment encourage these cracks to enlarge leading to failure. The stress of the abutment screw when tightened contributes to these tensional forces. When breakage occurs patients will require immediate attention, in aesthetic areas. With a delay of more than a few hours, the soft tissue will have closed over the implant. These unscheduled appointments are difficult to manage and the costs to replace the restorations are high.

With thin tissues and show-through of the abutment, colour is an issue; an alternative to all-ceramic abutments is to have porcelain fired onto the labial portion of an abutment that has been cast in a metal-ceramic alloy. Care must be taken to ensure that during the fabrication stages of this type of abutment, there is a layer of wax over the machined restorative cylinder so that a metal-ceramic alloy will be available to enamel porcelain. The machined cylinders in general are not receptive to porcelain bonding.

Gold custom abutments are the best compromise at present; yellow gold is strong in thin sections and can be cast easily to form. It also has a long record in dentistry of biocompatibility. Unless special circumstances are present, the gold custom abutment designed to support the soft tissue exit and follow the mucosal margin is most often chosen when screw retention is contra-indicated. Recently, several implant manufacturers (3i, Atlantis) offer custom abutments machined out of titanium coat titanium abutments with titanium nitride. This will give a golden hue to the abutment and should improve the aesthetics of the soft tissues when titanium abutments are used.

NINE

PROVISIONAL RESTORATIONS

For ideal aesthetics, a provisional restoration is required to shape and mold the soft tissue. A screw-retained provisional restoration is the easiest to use. It can be placed with ease as the screw can be used to seat the provisional and expand peri-implant mucosa. With screw-retained provisionals, the provisional restoration can be incorporated into the master impression to transfer information about the contours of the restoration to the technician. These procedures are not so easily accomplished with cemented restorations when surgical modifications to the soft tissues are required. It is difficult to manage the bleeding and cement a provisional restoration for ideal tissue health.

A tooth or implant-supported provisional restoration is often the preferred option. It offers psychological benefit and convenience for the patient and the clinician has control over the amount of soft tissue pressure exerted. A tissue borne removable prosthesis is indicated for its lower cost or in cases where no fixed support is available but the fitting surface of the tissue borne prosthesis has to be carefully adjusted to avoid violation of healing.

Different types of provisional restorations should be considered depending on the treatment modality prescribed. For instance, treatment involving complex bone regeneration and grafting techniques requires longer uninterrupted healing time and hence a provisional restoration that is durable and allows for easy modification is advantageous. On the other hand, implant placement with immediate provisionalisation requires a provisional restoration that can support the peri-implant tissues. The predictability of implant dentistry has shifted the therapy emphasis on not only the replacement of teeth but also the restoration of aesthetics. In addition to providing interim function, provisional restorations also serve as a template for the definitive restorations, and multiple sets of provisional restorations may be called for to formulate the best blueprint for the definitive restorations. CAD/CAM prostheses are ideal alternatives where multiple sets of provisional prostheses are anticipated to fit the various treatment stages. The digital data acquired can be saved and modified accordingly and prostheses can be manufactured without repeated impression and inconvenience to the patients.

Types of Provisional Restorations

Provisional restorations for implant dentistry may be broadly categorized into removal and fixed provisional restorations. Removable provisional restorations are generally tooth and/or soft tissue borne whereas fixed provisional restorations are supported by adjacent teeth or implants. Provisional restorations may be used immediately following a tooth extraction, during socket healing and site development, prior to implant placement and during osseointegration. Provisional restorations can also be used following implant uncovering for the purpose of soft tissue support, and aesthetics and function assessment prior to the delivery of the final restorations.

Removable Provisional Restorations, Removable partial prosthesis

An acrylic resin-based removable partial prosthesis (Acrylic-RPP) is commonly prescribed as a provisional prosthesis for its fabrication simplicity, cost, and ease of insertion. The ability to modify it to accommodate changes in ridge anatomy as a consequence of extraction, soft/hard tissue augmentation, and implant placement is also an advantage. However, their bulkiness, palatal coverage and removable nature are often the cited reasons for dissatisfaction by patients. The possibilities of initiating soft tissue inflammation around gingival margins and the potential of exerting pressure on the underlying surgical site are also causes of concern for clinicians. It is crucial that the removable prostheses should remain passive during the initial healing phase following soft/ hard tissue augmentation procedures and following implant placement as mucosal pressure could risk flap dehiscence, membrane exposure and bacterial contamination whereas micro-movement may lead to fibrous encapsulation of the dental implants. The creation of space between the prosthesis and the underlying tissue is sometimes necessary to minimize transmucosal pressure leading to an unsightly gap between the ridge and neck of the denture teeth.

Cobalt chromium-based removable partial prosthesis (CoCr-RPP) may be designed to be supported by teeth and therefore eliminate the problems associated with the tissue borne acrylic resin-based RPP. However, the additional fabrication cost and their inherent removable nature do not warrant their frequent use. However, the patient's existing CoCr-RPP may be modified to serve as the provisional prosthesis.

Vacuum-formed retainer

Vacuum-formed retainers often referred to as the Essix retainers, can be fabricated from clear thermoplastic sheets under high pressure and heat to retain pontics for missing teeth. The matrix for the vacuum form is made with a pre-extraction stone cast, a duplicate cast of the diagnostic wax-up of the missing teeth or a stone cast with denture teeth placed at the edentulous site. The tooth colour resin is used to fill the space after the retainer is made whereas denture teeth are captured inside the vacuumed form during thermal suction. The retainers are easy and inexpensive to fabricate and they are able to protect the healing site, as they are tooth-borne.

However, vacuum-formed retainers may not be appropriate for long-term use. As the occlusal surface of the entire arch is covered, the retainers may interfere with speech and mastication and may be aesthetically unacceptable by some patients. Partial arch coverage is not recommended as it may lead to occlusal interference or possible supra-eruption of uncovered teeth. Their durability is also limited as the thermoplastic material is vulnerable to occlusal wear and frequent replacement is often needed.

Fixed Provisional Restorations, Chairside resin bonded provisional restoration

A fixed provisional restoration offers psychological benefits and convenience for the patients and protects the surgical site from transmucosal pressure. Where the edentulous span is small and the provisional phase is short, bonding artificial teeth or a patient's extracted teeth to the adjacent natural teeth provide an easy and economical option. However, the bulk interproximal composite may result in unacceptable aesthetic outcomes for some patients and the composite junctions are vulnerable to fracture. Mesh plates or fibre strips can be incorporated to reinforce the composite bridge and reduce the need for bulky interproximal composite. It has the advantage that it can easily be detached and replaced onto the brackets throughout the treatment. However, the presence of brackets may be considered unsightly for some patients.

Laboratory made resin-bonded fixed partial prosthesis

When extended healing time is anticipated, cast metal-reinforced resin-bonded fixed partial prosthesis (FPP) may be considered for their structural durability. They were developed as a conservative option for definitive tooth replacement, and have since become popular as provisional prostheses for implant therapy. However, optimal aesthetics may be difficult to achieve because thin or translucent teeth are often unable to mask the grey colour of the palatal metal retainers.

All ceramic resin bonded FPP for missing anterior teeth may be used in selective patients when the aesthetic need is high during the provisional phase, the brittle nature of the ceramics does not permit intact removal for reuse whereas removal by mechanical tapping and recommendation is possible with metal-based prostheses.

Conventional fixed provisional restoration

Where teeth adjacent to surgical sites are indicated for complete coverage restorations, conventional fixed provisional restorations involving tooth preparation offer a convenient and predictable option without compromising the implant site. Where multiple periodontally compromised teeth are indicated for extraction for implant placement, sequential treatment with serial extraction concept may be employed. The periodontally compromised teeth are strategically selected and prepared as abutments for provisional prostheses and the remaining periodontally compromised teeth are extracted and replaced with implants. The healing and osseointegration are protected by the fixed provisional prostheses as transmucosal pressures are eliminated. Once the implants are integrated and uncovered, the abutment teeth are extracted and replaced with more implants if indicted and the provisional prosthesis is converted to be supported by the integrated implants via relining intra-orally with auto polymerizing resin.

In addition to the elimination of harmful pressure at surgical sites, conventional provisional FPP can be mechanically retained by temporary cement; and removal for modification and reuse is relatively easy compared to the resin bonded restorations. However, the polymethylmethacrylate resin used for the fabrication of the provisional prosthesis is prone to fracture without reinforcement in long-span situations. Loosening of the prosthesis, dentine sensitivity and secondary caries are some other possible complications.

Transitional implants

Provisional restorations supported by immediately loaded transitional implants (TI) offer a viable alternative to avoid any transmucosal loading in cases where a tooth-supported provisional restoration is not possible. TIs enable patients to use a provisional fixed restoration with form and function similar to those of the definitive prosthesis, at the same allows for uninterrupted healing at the implant and/or grafted site.

TIs can be placed in the edentulous sites before the ridge augmentation procedures or adjacent to the sites of the definitive implant placement. These implants are immediately loaded after a chairside reline of the interim removable partial dentures or polycarbonate crowns using auto polymerizing resin. Although these implants have been used with great success, excessive loading on TIs may result in their fracture. Moreover, placement of Tls too close to the definitive fixtures may prevent complete integration of the implant and the surrounding hard tissues.

Implant-Supported Provisional Restoration

Following the uncovering of the implants, provisional restorations are often prescribed to support the peri-implant tissues and to assess the aesthetic outcome of the treatment thus far. The provisional restoration is used to evaluate if the future definitive restoration is in harmony with surrounding structures and to detect if any hard and soft tissues deficiency is present. The relationship between the provisional restoration and surrounding structures dictates the need for further corrective surgeries and grafting procedures or prosthetic means to overcome the insufficiency in hard and soft tissue.

In optimal situations where no further corrective procedures are indicated, provisional restorations can shape the emergence profile of the restorations, and the matured soft tissue contour can be transferred to the definitive restorations with customized impression copings.

CAD/CAM Provisional Prostheses

With the advance in digital dentistry, CAD/CAM (computer-aided design/computer-aided manufacture) is now gaining popularity for manufacturing prostheses. The construction of a CAD/CAM prosthesis starts with data acquisition involving the construction of a digital model using a dental scanner based on a direct intra-oral scan or scanning an impression or a stone model of the patient. The prosthesis is designed virtually using a CAD program, which is then realized by processing with a milling machine, using the subtractive method or a 3-D printing machine, using the additive method. Prostheses made from the subtractive method are milled from solid blocks of materials but such method has the inherent shortcomings of excessive material wastage and the impossibility of reproducing undercuts. The additive method, utilizing the rapid prototyping (RP) technique, does not create excessive waste as the materials used are in powder or liquid forms which are then hardened by eternal power source sand layered into the final prosthesis. The most common technologies employed for additive methods in dentistry are stereolithography (SLA) and selective laser sintering (SLS) methods.

CAD/CAM technology can be used for the fabrication of provisional restorations employing high-density polymers based on highly cross-linked polymethylmethacrylate (PMMA) or composite resin. They allow for an extended provisionalisation phase as the high-density polymers used offer favourable mechanical behaviours and biocompatibility compared to the traditional indirect provisional prostheses. The ability to design and modify the pontic morphology digitally to accommodate for the changes in soft tissue architecture throughout the treatment.

TYPES OF ABUTMENTS FOR CEMENT RETENTION

The abutments for cement retention are of two types, one-piece abutment and two-piece abutment

A one-piece implant incorporates the trans-mucosal abutment as an integral part of the implant. It is often used with a flapless procedure and immediate loading (the crown is placed in a short time after placing the implant).

One-piece abutment advantages are:

- No need for a torque wrench
- No screw loosening
- The abutment does not engage the hexagon of the implant body and eliminates the risk of incomplete seating.
- No need to retighten under restoration
- Less expensive
- Thicker walls

Disadvantages are:

- The post may loosen and rotate because it does not engage the anti-rotational system
- Cannot be used for angled abutments
- Torque applied usually gets transferred to the bone crest
- Since it has a small diameter (2-2.5 mm) retention is a problem

TWO-PIECE ABUTMENT has one component (abutment) that engages an anti-rotational feature of the implant and another component (abutment screw) fixates the implant abutment and implant together. It can be used in almost all situations for a single tooth implant. There are two categories of the two-piece abutment designs, these are stock, pre-manufactured abutments and a laboratory customized abutment. Stock, pre-manufactured abutments can be a straight abutment or an angled abutment.

Angled abutments Off-axis implant placement can sometimes be compensated with angled abutments that still allow screw retention. For these angled abutments to be used the angle compensation must be more than 17 degrees. This is to allow sufficient divergence in the trajectory of the abutment screws to still allow housing for the retentive screw of the restoration. If the divergence of the implant axis and the retaining screw of the abutment to receive the restoration is less than 17 degrees, there remains insufficient bulk of the abutment to house the retaining screw of the restoration. In these situations, conventional screw retention of restorations is not possible. Lingual set screws can be incorporated to retain restorations on, essentially, abutments designed for cement retention, but these are technically challenging to execute.

Methods to displace cemented implant restorations include - One design used screws to displace cemented crowns by pushing against abutments. Abutments for this type of restoration were designed to receive cemented restorations, screws were incorporated into the restorations, and when needed the screws were activated to lift restorations off abutments.

The ideal abutment design should have the following characteristics:

1. The cement margin should follow the mucosal outline
2. The material of the abutment should be strong in a thin section
3. The material should be biocompatible.

<u>Cement margin</u>

Abutments to receive cemented implant restorations can be largely classified as stock or custom abutments. Stock abutments are fabricated by manufacturers and the cement margin and profile of the abutment are either made to average dimensions or ignored entirely.

The ideal implant position to obtain an aesthetic outcome will be located 3 mm or more below the buccal mucosal margin. When there is any scallop this can lead to the margin being 5-6 mm submucosal in the interproximal areas. The form of the margin of a cemented restoration conforms to the abutment margin. This deep margin leads to two clinical problems: maintaining the soft tissue profile while the restoration is removed, and cement removal after cementation. When a provisional restoration has been removed the tissue profile is held by the restoration and not by the abutment. If the restoration was not replaced within a short period the soft tissue would rapidly collapse around the abutment. In addition, cement can be seen at the restoration abutment interface. Removing this cement in deep sub-mucosal areas is difficult. Stock abutments should be used only when minimal scallop of the mucosal margins are present and cement margins can be kept within 2-3 mm of 68 the cement margin or stock abutments with supra-mucosal margins to be modified, to adapt more closely to mucosal margins to facilitate cement removal. Custom abutments are either waxed onto machined cylinders to form and cast or machined from titanium via a computer-aided design, or copied from a waxed form. When custom abutments are designed with the support of the soft tissue and cement margin location in mind, most of the problems of cementation with stock abutments can be overcome.

Strength of the abutment

The ideal abutment should be tooth coloured; this will allow ideal soft tissue colouration and the best opportunity for aesthetics, as all-ceramic restorations can be used. At present alumina or zirconia abutments are available. When the abutment retaining screw access and angle correction is taken into account, the resulting abutments are often left with very thin sections. These abutments are at risk of fracture due to these dimensions. Moreover, porcelain fails with crack propagation, and tensional forces in a wet environment encourage these cracks to enlarge leading to failure. The stress of the abutment screw when tightened contributes to these tensional forces. When breakage occurs patients will require immediate attention, especially in aesthetic areas. With a delay of more than a few hours, the soft tissue will have closed over the implant. These unscheduled appointments are difficult to manage and the costs to replace the restorations are high.

The restorations with ceramic abutments should be limited to single units, keeping in mind that they may fracture and require remaking the restoration. If multiple unit splints were built on ceramic abutments, a fracture of one abutment would cause the failure of the entire splint. Another consideration is the management of ceramic abutments in the event of screw loosening. With metallic abutments, restorations can sometimes be removed with pneumatic back action devices (Kavo coronoflex) and abutment screws can be re-torqued and restorations re-cemented. The use of these impact devices will cause fracture of the all-ceramic restorations and their abutments. With thin tissues and show-through of the abutment, colour is an issue; an alternative to all-ceramic abutments is to have porcelain fired onto the labial portion of an abutment that has been cast in a metal-ceramic alloy. Care must be taken to ensure that during the fabrication stages of this type of abutment, there is a layer of wax over the machined restorative cylinder so that a metal-ceramic alloy will be available to enamel porcelain. The machined cylinders in general are not receptive to porcelain bonding.

Biocompatibility

The most compatible materials for soft tissue are alumina and machined titanium. Another study found that abutments once in place should be left in place. Insertion and removal of the abutment have the potential to alter soft tissue levels and this may have an impact on the aesthetic outcome. While these findings should be kept in mind and these two materials have been shown to be suitable materials with respect to biocompatibility, the weakness of alumina and the grey colour of machined titanium can cause discolouration of the tissues. A ceramic abutment has the drawback of potential fracture and the titanium abutment has the potential to discolour tissue.

Gold custom abutments seem to be the best compromise at present; yellow gold is strong in thin sections and can be cast easily to form, and gold has a long record in dentistry of biocompatibility. Unless special circumstances are present, the gold custom abutment designed to support the soft tissue exit and follow the mucosal margin is most often chosen when screw retention is contra-indicated. Recently, several implant manufacturers (3i, Atlantis) that offer custom abutments machined out of titanium have advertised the capability of coating titanium abutments with titanium nitride. This will give a golden hue to the abutment and should improve the aesthetics of the soft tissues when titanium abutments are used. Other colours are also available with this coating, the effects of different coatings with respect to soft tissue discolouration. For example, a pink hue might be better than a golden hue for aesthetics.

The disadvantages of angled abutments are:

- Angled abutments are usually 15 to 30 degrees off-axis of the implant body which leads to a greater shear component of the load and screw loosening or fracture of the abutment.
- The metal thickness on the side of an angled abutment decreases which increases the risk of fracture
- The thin aspect of the angled abutment also prevents preparation and reduction of the abutment when the implant is too facial. Hence, an implant body that is too facial is made even worse when the angled abutment with a flare is placed.
- Manufacturers usually increase the abutment flare on angled abutments in order to increase the thickness of metal.

Laboratory customized abutment

The most widely used custom abutment is a plastic pattern that is waxed for contour and height and cast in precious metal. The advantage is the reduced cost. A disadvantage is that it is less precise and associated with a higher risk of abutment screw loosening.

PRE MACHINED TITANIUM SLEEVE COMPONENT

- The laboratory waxes onto the metal sleeve and casts precious alloy onto the machined coping.
- The primary advantage of the approach is the accuracy of fit for the hexagon engagement and the abutment screw head.
- As a result, the screw connection is more secure, and the risk of screw loosening is decreased.
- The disadvantage of this component is that the union between the titanium alloy and precious metal casting is not chemical and may lead to crevice breakdown and fracture.

CEMENT RETAINED IMPLANT PROSTHESIS

1. A complete arch closed tray impression is made using the indirect transfer coping assembly.

2. The implant analogue is screwed to the transfer coping and a cast using Type IV stone is poured.

3. The friction fit abutment is attached to the implant analogue

4. The abutment for a metal-ceramic crown is prepared

5. The hexagonal screwdriver is placed in a position to maintain the screw access channel. Make a wax pattern for the implant crown coping and is cast using a high noble metal-ceramic gold alloy.

6. The fit of the completed casting is verified intraorally.

7. The ceramic is added incrementally keeping the occlusal screw access channel open

8. Using the crown as a repositioning device, the abutment is screwed to the implant. The hexagonal screwdriver is passed through the open screw access channel.

9. Tighten and torque the abutment screw.

10. The crown is cemented with a definitive cement, such as zinc phosphate, glass ionomer, or resin cement. The excess cement is expressed through the access opening with an explorer. The screw channel is closed with gutta-percha and the occlusal surface is sealed with a composite.

11. When the access to remove excess cement is difficult, the following procedure is followed :

a. In step 8, the abutment screw is tightened with fingers only. Do not torque the abutment screw.

b. After definitive cementation, the hexagonal screwdriver is passed through the screw access channel. Loosen the abutment screw and remove the abutment with the prosthesis.

c. Visually inspect and any excess cement is removed.

d. The crown and abutment is repositioned. Torque the abutment screw and re-evaluate the occlusion.

FACTORS AFFECTING RETENTION OF CEMENT RETAINED RESTORATIONS

There are several factors that affect the retention of cement-retained restorations, these are:

A. TAPER :

The taper of an implant abutment affects the amount of retention. The retention of a crown rapidly decreases as the taper is increased from 6 to 25 degrees. Machined abutments have mostly 6 degree of taper depending on the concept of ideal tapering proposed by Jorgensen for natural teeth. Parallelism of axial walls has been recognized to be the single effective factor for retention

B. ABUTMENT SURFACE AREA:

The surface area of an implant abutment influences the amount of retention. Wider abutment offers greater retention than a narrow abutment. The greater diameter abutment has advantages of providing a greater taper, a thicker outer body wall and more surface area for retention.

C. ABUTMENT HEIGHT:

A tall preparation provides greater retention than a short abutment. The minimum abutment height to use cement-retained restorations with predictable retention was documented to be 5 mm.Therefore, when the inter occlusal space is as little as 4 mm, screw retained restorations may be used, since these restorations can be attached directly to implants without intermediate abutment.

D. SURFACE ROUGHNESS:

Increases mechanical retention for cements is done by creating microretentive irregularities. By using diamond burs or grit blasting. However, because of the ideal 6 degree taper and long surface provided by implant abutments, there will usually be no need for roughening abutment surface to increase retention.

E. GEOMETRY OF ABUTMENT:

Manufactured implant abutments for cement are usually circular in cross-section, providing little resistance to shear forces, especially on individual, unsplinted crowns. A flat side on the implant abutment preparation decreases shear forces on the cement interface. Whenever possible, a preparation with one or two flat sides should be made on circular abutments for cemented prostheses.

TEN

ADVANTAGES OF SCREW RETAINED RESTORATIONS OVER CEMENT RETAINED RESTORATIONS

When using cement-retained implant restorations, many of the same principles used for conventional fixed prosthodontics for natural teeth can be applied. Sufficient implant abutment dimensions (principally the height) are required for adequate retention of the crown. In situations where minimal interocclusal space exists or the implant is severely malaligned, it may not be possible to achieve adequate retention to retain the restoration with cement. However, fixture-level screw-retained restorations can be restored predictably with as little as 4 mm of space from the implant fixture to the occluding surface of the opposing dentition. In some situations, this can avoid pre-prosthetic surgery and invasive restorative treatment in an attempt to gain more restorative space for the implants.

Gingival molding is a critical step during the healing period to achieve satisfactory esthetics with natural-looking tissue profiles around implant crowns. A provisional restoration is required for this process as healing abutments do not have the proper size or emergence profile that the restoration needs. A screw-retained provisional restoration can be used with ease to incrementally expand the peri-implant tissues until fully seated. In addition, following implant surgeries where the provisional restoration is to be placed immediately, a screw-retained option is the preferred method; it is difficult to manage the bleeding and cement a restoration in a clean environment for ideal tissue health. Another advantage of an 80 screw-retained provisional restoration is that it can be used as a pick-up type impression coping. A soft tissue cast is poured around the exposed provisional after an impression coping is attached, yielding a soft tissue cast that is identical to the soft tissue form intraorally. This provides the laboratory with a model of an exact replica of the emergence profile that should be transferred to the definitive restoration. A screw-retained provisional has several advantages over cemented provisionals in achieving ideal tissue contours, maintaining tissue health, and transferring the soft tissue profile in an impression for laboratory communication.

Peri-implant tissues around screw-retained restorations present with fewer biological complications. In vitro studies demonstrate that cement-retained prostheses luted to titanium abutments with simulated margins have been shown to leave a large number of cement remnants. When restorations are luted to the implant abutment, extruded cement has enough hydraulic pressure to tear the delicate tissues surrounding the implant instead of being deflected out. With the surfaces of newer implants purposefully roughened for better healing, cement is expected to have even greater adherence and cleaning becomes significantly more challenging. This is of even greater importance in an immediate loading situation where there is often space between the wall of the extraction site and the implant body where cement could flow. However, the problem was associated only with screw-retained single crowns that had loose abutment screws creating a micro gap. The inflammation healed soon after the retightening of the screws once the gap was closed. When properly interfaced, the gap distance between the machine-surfaced implant and abutment is superior to any cement margin that can be developed. A screw-retained interface will allow less bacterial penetration and fewer peri-implant complications will be seen. A screw-retained restoration demonstrates fewer biologic complications compared to cement-retained prostheses. Cement extrusion and retention in the peri-implant tissues can result in microbial colonization and soft/hard tissue damage.

When treatment planning with implants in partially edentulous patients, the clinician should always assess the prognosis of the remaining teeth, especially for teeth adjacent to proposed implants. In the case of teeth with a poor or questionable prognosis next to implants, the implant restoration should always be designed with the eventual loss of those teeth in mind. Implant restoration can always be modified and used to support new pontics in the future, should the teeth require extraction. However, it takes strategic planning of metal framework designs. Recycling and addition to an existing prosthesis are simplified with screw-retained 81 restorations as they can be removed intact. Cement-retained restorations are often extensively damaged beyond repair during the removal process. When a complication arises for removal of the prosthesis, a screw-retained prosthesis will simplify the management process.

COMPLICATIONS

1. Porcelain Fracture:

Implants do not have a periodontal ligament therefore, higher forces are exerted on crowns. As a consequence, porcelain fracture is quite a common complication. Because some porcelain may be left unsupported due to the screw access channel, screw-retained prostheses are even more susceptible to porcelain fracture. In an attempt to minimize this problem, the use of a metal occlusal table is gaining popularity, especially in areas with heavy occlusal loads, limited vertical clearance, and without esthetic concerns.

2. Peri-Implant Tissue Inflammation:

Residual cement is a common complication of cement-retained prostheses. The shape of the abutment and crown must follow the soft tissue to prevent cement margins that are too deep. Soft tissue inflammation and bone loss can occur when residual cement is left. Therefore, it is important to remove all excess cement at the time of crown insertion. Techniques to ease cement removal, involve placing petroleum jelly on the outer surface of the crown, the use of curettes to carefully scale around the crown, and the meticulous use of dental floss. This is not a problem with a screw-retained prosthesis because no cement is used. Peri-implant soft tissue responses are more favourable with screw-retained restorations compared with cement-retained restorations. However, there have been reports of gingival inflammation because of the micro gap between the restoration and the abutment interface. A study performed by Piattelli et al showed bacterial infiltration in the screw-retained implant assembly because of the micro gap compared with no bacterial or fluid penetration in the cement-retained implant assembly. The group concluded the superiority of cement-retained restorations in terms of fluid and bacterial permeability.

3. Screw Fracture/Loosening:

The main disadvantage observed with screw-retained restorations is the screw loosening that occurs during function. The incidence of screw loosening or fractures varies between 10% and 65% depending on the studies and the types of restorations. It occurs most frequently with single-tooth implant restorations, restorations in the molar area, and long cantilevers. The advent of newer implant systems (e.g., internal connections with a geometric lock, larger abutments, and screws designs) has greatly reduced the incidence of screw loosening as was seen with the traditional hexagonal implant systems. To prevent screw loosening, various techniques, such as the anti-rotational feature, direct mechanical interlock, changes in screw design, and torque controlling mechanisms with torque wrenches can be employed. A restoration that is both cemented and screwed retained known as the "Combination Implant Crown." offers the advantages of both worlds, such as esthetics, retrievability, and anti-rotational features with the octagon engagement. Detrimental forces including excursive, off-axis centric, interproximal, and cantilever contacts should be thoroughly evaluated and eliminated whenever possible. A more favourable distribution of the forces is obtained when the implant is placed parallel to the occlusal forces. A nonpassive framework also increases the likelihood of screw loosening. Another complication is the fatigue failure of the screw, because the screw holding the prosthesis has a narrow diameter, the strength of the prosthesis is compromised. Conversely, the components of the cement-retained restoration are mainly large and, therefore, fatigue failure does not occur often.

ELEVEN
DISCUSSION

The comparison of two different concepts of restoring implants with regard to prosthetic complications, peri-implant soft tissue conditions and peri-implant marginal bone levels were compared. Cross arch stabilisation on multiple implant splinting provides biomechanical advice in immediate loading cases, sharing the load between all implants and minimizing micromotion. Multiple units of screw-retained provisional restorations may lack passivity causing mechanical complications because of strain on the different components which is expressed as fractures in the weakest part of the prosthetic structure.

The use of cement space accommodates passivity and is one of the advantages of cement-retained restorations. In respect to implant position related considerations, cement-retained restorations can adjust to multiple implant positions, providing superior esthetics.

When screw-retained prostheses are used in an immediate loading procedure, the recall appointments should include retightening of the prosthesis, so that screw loosening and uncontrolled loading are prevented.

Nissan et al compared the long term outcome and complications of cemented versus screw-retained implant restorations in partially edentulous patients and concluded that the long term outcome of cemented implant-supported restorations was superior to that of screw-retained restorations both clinically and biologically.

Sheriff et al evaluated in a systemic review the survival and success rate of screw versus cement-retained implant crowns. There was no significant difference between cemented and screw-retained restorations for major and minor outcomes with regard to implant survival or crown loss.

A systematic review and meta-analysis conducted by Lemos C et al compared cement- and screw-retained retention systems in fixed implant-supported restorations in terms of marginal bone loss, implant survival, and prosthetic complications. The 20 studies selected for review evaluated 2139 participants, with a mean age of 47.14 years and who had received 8989 dental implants. The follow-up was 65.4 months. Results for marginal bone loss showed significant differences in favour of the cement-retained prosthesis. The implant survival rate was higher for the cement-retained prosthesis and the prosthetic complication rate was higher for the screw-retained prosthesis.

Polo GM et al compiled and enumerated all the factors described in the literature that may affect the decision to use either cemented or screw-retained restorations and to determine the relative weights of each factor by type of retention and prosthesis. The literature was reviewed, and the factors were classified as determining (present in a clinical situation in which one of the retention mechanisms was clearly more suitable than the other) or conditioning (present in clinical situations in which one type of restoration was not clearly more advantageous than the other). The results show that three determining factors (esthetic outcome, retention, and biologic risk) and five conditioning factors (passive fit, fracture strength, occlusal area, complications, and retrievability) were identified. Thus, the study concluded that there is no better alternative for all clinical situations, determining factors in certain scenarios can render one of the two approaches more recommendable. For esthetic reasons, when the implant angle cannot be corrected to conceal the access hole, cementation is more suitable; however, screw retention is the better option when the occlusal space is under 6 mm or margins cannot be located supra- or equigingivally. In the absence of determining factors, the decision should be based on conditioning factors, which carry different weights depending on the type of prosthesis.

Screw- and cement-retained implant prostheses both have advantages and disadvantages. A review of the literature shows that neither method can be used in every clinical situation, so it remains up to the clinician to make the most evidence-based decision as to which retention method will be most effective. Major risk factors to consider are porcelain-related failures (chipping or fracturing), screw loosening or fracture, and peri-implant disease secondary to residual excess cement in the peri-implant tissues. Retrievability should also be at the forefront of decision-making to be able to easily manage technical or biological complications. Angulated screw channels and dynamic abutments are making screw-retained restorations more versatile, especially in the anterior esthetic zone.

For single-crown restorations, screw-retained prostheses experienced more technical complications whereas cement-retained prostheses experienced more biological complications. The clinician must decide what he/she is willing to maintain more during follow-up visits. Full-arch implant restorations should be screw-retained. They are more easily retrieved for the management of technical complications and also seem preferable from a biological perspective.

TWELVE
CONCLUSION

The decision to restore an implant prosthesis with a cement-retained or a screw-retained design hinges on multiple factors. Clinicians should be aware of the limitations of each type of prosthesis so as to select the one that is most appropriate for the clinical situation. High-quality standards and precision ensure longevity for both screw and cement-retained restorations.

Conclusions and Clinical recommendations for screw retention:

Screw retention may be recommended

- In the presence of minimal interarch space (minimum 4 mm)
- For FDPs with a cantilever design
- For long-span FDPs
- To avoid an additional risk factor with the use of cement and a possible cement remnant
- In the esthetic zone, for provisionalization of implants to enable soft tissue conditioning and finalization of the emergence and mucosal profile
- When retrievability is desired

Implants must be placed in a prosthetically ideal position with the future access hole of the planned crown below the planned incisal edge in order to facilitate screw retention.

Conclusions and clinical recommendations for cement retention:

Cement retention may be recommended

- For short-span prostheses with margins at or above the mucosa, level
- To compensate for improperly inclined implants
- For cases where an easier control of occlusion without an access hole is desired – for example, with narrow-diameter crowns.

The cementation procedure should be carried out with great caution, with the FDP margins placed at or above the tissue level

THIRTEEN
REFERENCES

1. Dental Implant Prosthetics, 2nd edition, By Carl E. Misch

2. Dental Implant Prosthetics, 1st edition, By Carl E. Misch

3. Implant-supported prostheses – Vincente Jimenez Lopez

4. Implant prosthodontics – Fredrickson, Stevens, Gress

5. Dental Implants – Winkelman and Orth

6. Cementation Procedures for Dental Implants, Patterson Dental

7. Mohit Kheur et al. Clinical Considerations for Cementation of Implant Retained Restorations. IJDA 2010; 2(2): 180-181.

8. Buzayan MM et al. A simple procedure for retrieval of a cement-retained implant-supported crown: A case report, Quintessence Int.

9. Schoenbaum T.R. et al. Screw-Access Marking: A Technique to Simplify Retrieval of Cement-Retained Implant Prostheses, Compendium 2013; 34(3): 1-6.

10. Guichet D.L. et al. Passivity of Fit and Marginal Opening in Screw- or Cement-Retained Implant Fixed Partial Denture Designs. Int J Oral Maxillofac Implants 2000;15: 239–246.

11. Weber HP et al. Peri-implant soft-tissue health surrounding cement- and screw-retained implant restorations: a multi-centre, 3-year prospective study. Clin Oral Implants Res. 2006;17(4): 375-379.

12. Da Rocha et al. Influence of screw access on the retention of cement-retained implant prostheses. J Prosthet Dent 2013;109: 264-268.

13. Vigolo P et al. Cemented versus screw-retained implant-supported single-tooth crowns: a 4-year prospective clinical study. Int J Oral Maxillofac Implants. 2004 Mar-Apr;19(2): 260-265.

14. Nissan J et al. Long-Term Outcome of Cemented Versus Screw-Retained Implant-Supported Restorations. Int J Oral Maxfac Implants 2011;26: 1102–1107.

15. Julia-Gabriela Wittneben. Clinical Performance of Screw- Versus Cement-Retained Fixed Implant-Supported Reconstructions—A Systematic Review. Int J Oral MaxFac Implants 2014;29(suppl):84–98.

16. Stefania C. Kano et al. Effect of Casting Procedures on Screw Loosening in UCLA-Type Abutments. J Prosthodont 2006;15: 77-81.

17. Rola Shadid, Nasrin Sadaqa. A Comparison Between Screw- and Cement-Retained Implant Prostheses. A Literature Review. Journal of Oral Implantology Vol. XXXVIII/No. Three/2012.

18. Tsuyoshi Kitagawa, Yasuhiro Tanimoto, Misako Odaki, Kimiya Nemoto, Masahiro Aida. Influence of implant/ abutment joint designs on abutment screw loosening in a dental implant system. 2005 Wiley Periodicals, Inc. J Biomed Mater Res Part B: Appl Biomater 2005;75B: 457– 463.

19. Rosario Prisco, Steven M. Morgano, Salvatore D'Amato. New abutment for a screw-retained implant-supported crown. J Prosthet Dent 85(1); 30-33.

20. Lee A, Okayasu K, Wang HL. Screw- Versus Cement-Retained Implant Restorations: Current Concepts. Implant Dentistry, 19(1); 8-15.

21. Torrado E, Ercoli C, Mardini MA, Graser GN, Tallents RH, Cordaro L. A comparison of the porcelain fracture resistance of screw-retained and cement-retained implant-supported metal-ceramic crowns, JPD 91(6): 532-537.

22. Assenza B, Artese L, Scarano A, et al. Screw vs cement-implant-retained restorations: An experimental study in the beagle. Part 2. Immunohistochemical evaluation of the peri-implant tissues. J Oral Implantol 2006;32: 1–7.

23. Assenza B, Scarano A, Leghissa G, et al. Screw- vs cement-implant-retained restorations: an experimental study in the beagle. Part 1. Screw and abutment loosening. J Oral Implantol 2005;31: 242–247.

24. Arvidson K, Esselin O, Felle-Persson E, Jonsson G, Smedberg JI, Soderstrom U. Early loading of mandibular full-arch bridges screw-retained after 1 week to four to five Monotype implants: 3-year results from a prospective multicentre study. Clin Oral Implants Res 2008;19: 693–703.

25. Cho SC, Small PN, Elian N, Tarnow D. Screw loosening for standard and wide diameter implants in partially edentulous cases: 3- to 7-year longitudinal data. Implant Dent 2004;13: 245–250.

26. Crespi R, Vinci R, Cappare P, Romanos GE, Gherlone E. A clinical study of edentulous patients rehabilitated according to the "all on four" immediate function protocol. Int J Oral Maxillofac Implants 2012; 27: 428–434.

27. Schweitzer DM, Berg RW, Mancia GO. A technique for retrieval of cement-retained implant-supported prostheses. J Prosthet Dent 2011; 106(2): 134-138.

28. Al-Omari WM, Shadid R, Abu-Naba'a L, Massoud BE. Porcelain fracture resistance of screw-retained, cement-retained, and screw-cement-retained implant-supported metal-ceramic posterior crowns. J Prosthodont 2010;19: 263-273.

29. Recani B, Dulcic N, Cimic S, Catic A. Periodontal pathogens in screw and cement-retained prosthetic appliances. Annu Res Rev Biol 2014;15: 2450-2461.

30. Schoenbaum TR, Chang YY, Klokkevold PR. Screw-access marking: a technique to simplify retrieval of cement-retained implant prostheses. Compend Contin Educ Dent 2013;34: 230-236.

31. Schoenbaum T, Wadhwani C. screw-retained versus cement-retained restorations: aesthetic zone options. Dent Today 2017; 36(1): 1-7.

32. Ochoa D, Stanley K, Jovanovic S. A new approach for screw-retained restorations. Journal of Cosmetic Dentistry, 2015; 30(4): 94-101.

33. Polo MG, Ortega R, Polo GC, Celemin A, Highsmith JDR. Factors affecting the decision to use cemented or screw-retained fixed implant-supported prostheses: a critical review. Int J Prosthodont 2017; 1-12.

34. Wittneben JG, Joda T, Weber HP, Bragger U. Screw retained vs. cement-retained implant-supported fixed dental prosthesis. Periodontology 2000; 73(1): 141-151.

35. Crespi R, Capparè P, Gastaldi G, Gherlone EF. Immediate occlusal loading of full-arch rehabilitations: screw-retained versus cement-retained prosthesis. An 8-year clinical evaluation. Int J Oral Maxillofac Implants 2014; 29(6): 1406-1411.

36. Nissan J, Narobai D, Gross O, Ghelfan O, Chaushu G. Long-term outcome of cemented versus screw-retained implant-supported partial restorations. Int J Oral Maxillofac Implants 2011; 26(5):1102-1107.

37. Al Dosari AAF, Habib SR, Alnassar T, Alshihri A, Kamalan R. The current considerations in the fabrication of implant prostheses and the state of prosthetic complications: A survey among the dental technicians. Saudi Dent J. 2018; 30(4): 299-305.

38. Hameed MH, Khan FR, Ghafoor R, Azam SI. Marginal bone loss around cement and screw-retained fixed implant prosthesis. J Clin Exp Dent 2018;10(10): e949-e954.

39. Kheur M, Harianawala H, Kantharia N, Sethi T, Jambhekar S. Access to abutment screw in cement-retained restorations: a clinical tip. J Clin Diagn Res. 2015; 9(2): ZD17-18. 89

40. Fischer K, Stenberg T. Prospective 10-year cohort study based on a randomized, controlled trial (RCT) on implant-supported full-arch maxillary prostheses. Part II: Prosthetic outcomes and maintenance. Clin Implant Dent Relat Res 2011 Aug 11.

41. Linkevicius T, Vindasiute E, Puisys A, Peciuliene V. The influence of margin location on the amount of undetected cement excess after delivery of cement-retained implant restorations. Clin Oral Implants Res 2011; 22: 1379–1384.

42. Armellini D, Bilko S, Carmichael RP, von Fraunhofer JA. Screw-retained prosthesis for Straumann implant sites with limited interocclusal clearance. J Prosthodont. 2006; 15(3): 198-201.

43. Goodacre CJ, Bernal G, Rungcharassaeng K, Kan JY. Clinical complications with implants and implant prostheses. J Prosthet Dent 2003; 90: 121–132.

44. McRory ME, Cagna DR. A technique for fabricating single screw-retained implant-supported interim crowns in conjunction with implant surgery. J Prosthet Dent. 2014;111:455–9.

45. Antal MA, Csak C, Simon Fiala D, Braunitzer G. Rehabilitation with all-on-four and all-on-six using a variable thread profile implant system: short-term success and associated bone loss.

46. M Taruna, B Chittaranjan, N Sudheer, Suchita Tella, and Md. Abusaad. Prosthodontic Perspective to All-On-4® Concept for Dental Implants. J Clin Diagn Res. 2014; 8(10): ZE16–ZE19.

47. M. Gargari, V. Prete, A. Pujia, F.M. Ceruso. Full-arch maxillary rehabilitation fixed on 6 implants. Oral Implantol (Rome). 2013; 6(1): 1–4.

48. Bhering CLB, Mesquita MF, Kemmoku DT, Noritomi PY, Consani RLX, Barao VAR. Comparison between all-on-four and all-on-six treatment concepts and framework material on stress distribution in the atrophic maxilla: A prototyping guided 3D-FEA study. Materials Science and Engineering C 69(2016) 715-725.

49. Chee W, Jivraj S. Designing abutments for cement-retained implant-supported restorations. Br Dent J. 2006; 201(9): 559-563.

50. Cappare P, Sannino G, Minoli M, Montemezzi P, Ferrini F. Conventional versus Digital Impressions for Full-Arch Screw-Retained Maxillary Rehabilitation: A Randomized Clinical Trial. Int J Environ Res Public Health. 2019; 16(5): 829.

51. Sheriff S, Susarla SK, Kapos T, Munoz D, Chang BM, Wright RF. A systematic review of screw versus cement-retained implant-supported fixed restorations. J Prosthodont 2013.

52. Jivraj S. Screw versus cemented implant restorations: The decision-making process. J Dent Implant 2018; 8: 9-19.

53. S. Kourtis. Impression techniques for implant restorations. Dental Implants. 2018. www. Avid science.com

9 798885 695190

Printed by Libri Plureos GmbH in Hamburg,
Germany